USER EXPERIENCE RESEARCH

USER EXPERIENCE RESEARCH

DISCOVER WHAT CUSTOMERS REALLY WANT

MARTY GAGE AND SPENCER MURRELL

WILEY

No part of this publication may be reproduced, stored in a retrieval system, or transmitted in any form or by any means, electronic, mechanical, photocopying, recording, scanning, or otherwise, except as permitted under Section 107 or 108 of the 1976 United States Copyright Act, without either the prior written permission of the Publisher, or authorization through payment of the appropriate per-copy fee to the Copyright Clearance Center, Inc., 222 Rosewood Drive, Danvers, MA 01923, (978) 750-8400, fax (978) 750-4470, or on the web at www.copyright.com. Requests to the Publisher for permission should be addressed to the Permissions Department, John Wiley & Sons, Inc., 111 River Street, Hoboken, NJ 07030, (201) 748-6011, fax (201) 748-6008, or online at http://www.wiley.com/go/permission.

Limit of Liability/Disclaimer of Warranty: While the publisher and author have used their best efforts in preparing this book, they make no representations or warranties with respect to the accuracy or completeness of the contents of this book and specifically disclaim any implied warranties of merchantability or fitness for a particular purpose. No warranty may be created or extended by sales representatives or written sales materials. The advice and strategies contained herein may not be suitable for your situation. You should consult with a professional where appropriate. Further, readers should be aware that websites listed in this work may have changed or disappeared between when this work was written and when it is read. Neither the publisher nor authors shall be liable for any loss of profit or any other commercial damages, including but not limited to special, incidental, consequential, or other damages.

For general information on our other products and services or for technical support, please contact our Customer Care Department within the United States at (800) 762-2974, outside the United States at (317) 572-3993 or fax (317) 572-4002.

Wiley also publishes its books in a variety of electronic formats. Some content that appears in print may not be available in electronic formats. For more information about Wiley products, visit our web site at www.wiley.com.

Library of Congress Cataloging-in-Publication Data is Available:
ISBN: 9781119884217 (paperback)
ISBN: 9781119884224 (ePub)
ISBN: 9781119884231 (ePDF)

Cover Design and Image: Courtesy of the Authors
Developed by: Marty Gage, Spencer Murrell, Chris Rockwell
Written by: Marty Gage, Spencer Murrell
Designed by: Lisa Calvert, Lindsay Courtney, Vida Law, Jessica Rosenbaum, Steve Simula, Collin Simula, Pily Tamara
Contributing writers: Hannah Eber, Lauren Freese, Timmy Kusnierek
Inspired by: Dean Victor Ermoli, The Savannah College of Art and Design
Advised by: Professor Kwela Hermanns, The Savannah College of Art and Design
SKY10033197_032522

DEDICATED TO . . .

Everyone that has worked at Lextant, and anyone who has ever wondered how to conduct user research that inspires success.

Justine Gage for her instrumental role in defining and refining this approach for the last 17 years.

Kim Murrell for her inspiration and support.

We extend our gratitude to SCAD, the University for Creative Careers, for its partnership in the development of a curriculum and certification program that forms the basis of this book.

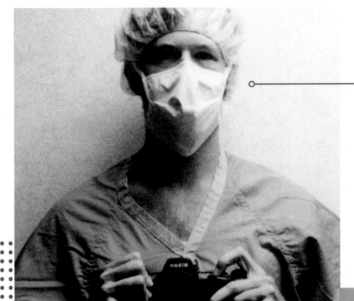

MARTY GAGE

Design Research

SPENCER MURRELL

Insight Translation

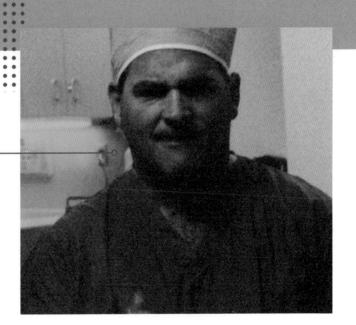

c1989

In the 80s, when I was in design school, my professors would tell us that half of all new product introductions failed in the market. I think this was intended to inspire us to find better ways of delivering new products to the market. The only advice they could offer at the time was to keep the end user at the center of the design process.

Now, forty years later, the numbers have changed very little. Some estimates suggest that the failure rate today is even higher.

Marty and I have worked together in numerous jobs honing an approach to research that hopes to eventually increase the success rate of new products. Our approach is a blend of art and science that attempts to answer the key questions that every designer asks when embarking on a project: How can I connect the things I design to a positive emotional connection with the end user?

It was not a quick or easy journey, but we are now at a place where we can confidently and repeatedly describe the design of a thing and its role in an experience.

In the following pages we will expose you to our philosophy and processes so that wherever you are in your career, you will be better equipped to succeed.

– Spencer Murrell

CONTENTS

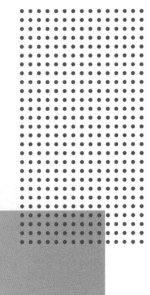

THE DESIGN THINKING PROCESS

We assume that you are familiar with this idea. This book is about the first step in the process, Empathize.

It's important to get this step right, because it is the foundation for everything that follows. You do not want to invest time and resources on ideas that have little to no value with users. Do not shortchange the first step.

THE DESIGN THINKING MODEL

D.SCHOOL

This five-stage Design Thinking model was initially proposed by the Hasso-Plattner Institute of Design at Stanford (design school). It was developed as a methodology to creatively solve complex problems.

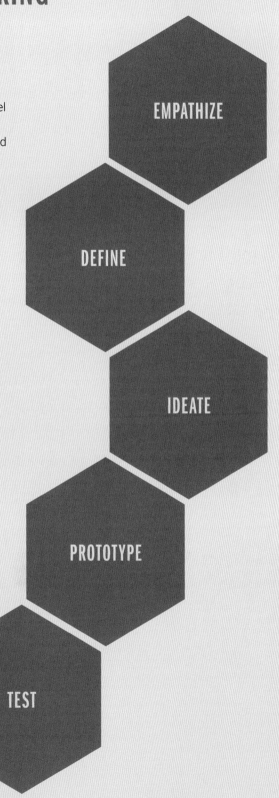

EMPATHIZE

DEFINE

IDEATE

PROTOTYPE

TEST

THE SIX KEY PRINCIPLES FOR SUCCESSFUL USER RESEARCH

These principles will help to guide your thinking and the research choices you make.

Ultimately you will be confident that you know what people really want, how to communicate it in a clear and engaging way, align teams around the problem to solve, and provide guardrails for the solution itself.

The principles will be referred to throughout the book.

SIX KEY PRINCIPLES

RELEVANT
Grounded in the desired business or social outcomes that are the reason for the design initiative. Learning objectives drive methodological choices.

ASPIRATIONAL
Focuses on understanding people's dreams for the future.

HOLISTIC
Thinks in terms of complete experiences. Connections are made between what needs to be designed and how it makes people feel.

RIGOROUS
Based on truth and reality. Seeks to minimize bias. Utilizes a repeatable process to support identifying patterns in the data. Guessing is eliminated.

ACTIONABLE
Clearly defines the problem to solve. Focuses and inspires creativity in a straightforward way. People know how to use it.

VISUAL
Utilizes imagery for engaging participants, telling the story, and concretely describing the problem to solve.

HOW TO USE THIS BOOK

This book contains all the tools to help practitioners approach the first phase in the Design Thinking process: Empathize. In order to provide this information in a systematic way, each chapter is set up in a consistent format.

PRINCIPLES

Each chapter includes an indication of which principles are the focus.

THINKING

Section 1 of each chapter explains the thought process behind that chapter.

TOOLS

Section 2 describes the tools used during that chapter.

EXECUTION

Section 3 explains how to execute successfully.

TOPIC

A single chapter covers an individual concept or step in our overall process.

CHAPTER 4:

HAVING EFFECTIVE CONVERSATIONS

1. **FORMULATE YOUR QUESTIONS**
The questions you ask a research participant should be directly related to your research objectives. You are going from a few big objectives to a detailed set of questions.

2. **CREATE A DISCUSSION GUIDE**
You want to have a structured plan for how you do your interviews. This tool puts all of your interview questions in a structure that flows.

3. **CONDUCT INTERVIEWS**
Moderation, or guiding a discussion, is a skill that you develop over the course of many conversations. Everyone has their own unique approach, and it takes a lot of practice to discover your own method that is not only effective at getting the data you need but also authentic to who you are.

REVIEW

The end of each chapter includes a review. This provides a summary for each section and the link back to our principles.

WHAT NEXT

We conclude the chapter with a few instructions on how to practice these skills and prepare for the next chapter.

CHAPTER 1:

Relevant Aspirational Holistic Rigorous Actionable Visual

MAKING EXPERIENCES ACTIONABLE

A USER-DRIVEN PERSPECTIVE ON DESIGN THINKING

There are many points of view on the design thinking process. You will learn how we think about it.

DEFINING VALUE: WHAT PEOPLE REALLY WANT

For ideas to be successful, other people need to find them valuable. You will learn to do research that helps generate ideas by soliciting the opinions of others.

IDEAL EXPERIENCE RESEARCH

You need to understand what people value in a way that informs your design. The research you conduct should be future-focused, aspirational, and actionable.

A USER-DRIVEN PERSPECTIVE ON DESIGN THINKING

The Design Thinking process is, by its nature, broad and generalized so that it can be applied to any design or business problem.

As we said, this book is about our approach to getting the first step right. However, we have learned from experience that what you learn in the first step must be applied in each subsequent step.

Based upon this requirement we redefined the phases to show how user experience research should be used at each step in the process. Each of these steps could be a book unto itself.

1. DEFINE VALUE

This step is about discovering what people really want. Defining what people value allows you to design something with the potential to deliver a truly meaningful experience.

2. DRIVE ALIGNMENT

First everyone on the team, and all stakeholders, must agree upon what people want. Once this agreement is achieved, they must decide and agree upon what to make. This is the problem your design will work to solve for the user. This is often referred to as a design brief.

3. FOCUS CREATIVITY

You know the experiences that people are seeking. You know what features you need to deliver. If your research was actionable, your ideas should flow.

4. PROTOTYPE EXPERIENCES

You want to embody your idea in a way that clearly communicates to people the experience your design will deliver.

5. MEASURE VALUE

You need to assess how well your design will deliver the experience people are seeking.

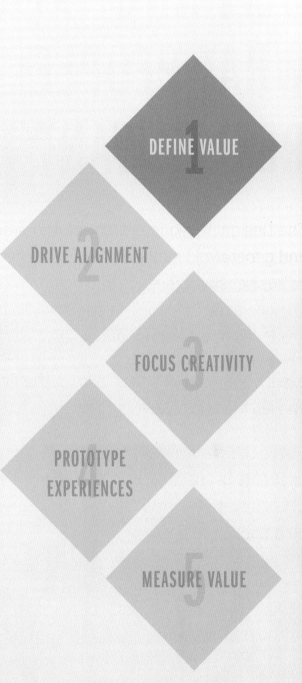

DEFINING VALUE: WHAT PEOPLE REALLY WANT

Defining value requires a structured process that, when followed, consistently yields success. The following chapters teach you how to make smart choices at each step. The choices you make will be grounded in the six key principles.

DEFINE VALUE 1

DEFINE OBJECTIVES

Clearly outline what goal your design needs to achieve, what you need to learn from users to meet that goal, and the type of deliverable you need to create to communicate what people want. *(see chapter 2 for details)*

DEVELOP AN APPROACH

Describe the people that will buy and use your design. Find and recruit some of these people to be your research participants.

Select the research approach that will deliver on your learning objectives. Develop, test, and refine your research methodology. *(see chapters 3, 4, 5, 6 & 7 for details)*

CONDUCT THE RESEARCH

Implement your research, in a repeatable manner, with your research participants. Capture the data. *(see chapters 4, 5, 6, 7 & 8 for details)*

ANALYZE THE DATA

Identify patterns. Develop themes from these patterns. *(see chapter 9 for details)*

INSIGHT TRANSLATION™

Create a one-page framework that concisely tells the story of what people want.

Embody your research findings in a clear, simple, and inspiring way. *(see chapters 9 & 10 for details)*

IDEAL EXPERIENCE RESEARCH

Ideal experiences are future-focused.
Many research techniques seek to understand the experiences people are having today as a way of providing inspiration for innovation. They rely on the pain points and barriers of today and limit their innovation potential.

Ideal experiences are aspirational.
We believe that innovation should be inspired by people's ideal experiences. People have aspirations for themselves – they dream of a perfect future. These are profound triggers that you can leverage to build strong relationships with customers. Understanding these triggers is crucial.

Ideal experiences are actionable.
We use the Anatomy of Experience Framework to describe experiences as an interrelated series of insights that work together to connect the desired emotions with specific design attributes. This connection allows you to understand how the design of a product or service can make emotional connections with people.

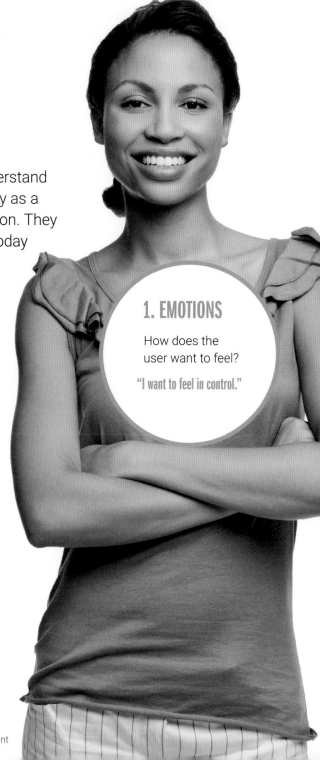

1. EMOTIONS

How does the user want to feel?

"I want to feel in control."

2. BENEFITS

What does the product or service do for the user?

"I am at ease."

I am focused because I don't feel like I'm rushed, holding up other people in line, or imposing on the tellers' time.

3. FEATURES

How is the benefit delivered?

"It is private."

It secludes me so I feel like no one can oversee or overhear my personal business.

4. SENSORY CUES

What are the signals that tell the user that the product or service will deliver?

"It has a secluded location."

It is in its own room, mini rooms, or pod with at least three walls and a door in a separate area of the bank or around the edge of the lobby.

THE ANATOMY OF EXPERIENCE FRAMEWORK

The Anatomy of Experience Framework is a tool we use to describe experiences. It is broken down into four interrelated categories: emotions, benefits, features, and sensory cues. These categories represent the information you need to understand in order to design something meaningful.

Emotions and benefits insights can be used to craft messaging while features and sensory cues insights are useful for design.

MESSAGING:

1. EMOTIONS

How do people want to feel?

——

Example:
I feel confident that my phone will never fail.

2. BENEFITS

What does your design have to provide in order to make people feel this way?

——

Example:
My phone will not break.

DESIGN:

3. FEATURES

How does your design deliver the benefits?

——

Example:
My phone is shockproof.

4. SENSORY CUES

What sensory cues do people associate with these features?

——

Example:
My phone has rubberized contact surfaces.

1. EMOTIONS

At the core of an experience is the emotional state of the user. Here the emphasis is on how something makes a person feel or how a person wants to feel when interacting with a product or service. These pictures express life or feelings about life. They are metaphorical.

To think emotionally, try completing the statement:

I FEEL . . .

RELAXED

I have no worries. Everything is taken care of.

ACCOMPLISHED

I have the tools I need to set it up so I can have my yay moment when it works.

Other ideal emotion examples include:

I FEEL . . .

Accomplished	Creative
Appreciated	Excited
Attractive	Free to be me
Cared For	In Control
Connected	Loved

PROUD

I want to be unique and stand out from the crowd.

IN CONTROL

I control how I treat my symptoms.

Nurturing	Successful	Courageous
Proud	Professional	Hopeful
Relaxed	Confident	Happy
Respected	Excited	Accepted
Safe	Encouraged	Free

2. BENEFITS

Once you understand how a person feels or wants to feel, it is important to understand "why." What is causing the person to feel that way? What is the current product or service doing or not doing to cause these feelings? What does the product or service need to do in order to enable this desired emotional state? This begins to uncover the benefits your design needs to deliver. These pictures communicate the impact that interacting with your design has on a person. They are metaphorical and tend to be in context.

To think about benefits, try completing the statement:

I AM . . .

READY TO TAKE ON THE DAY

I want a nutritional supplement that is always there for me, helping me stay fit, active, and healthy.

Other ideal benefit examples include:

I AM . . .

Getting Things Done	Helping My Loved Ones
Ready for the Day	Enjoying Time with Friends
Growing My Business	Helping My Family
Enjoying Time with Friends	Prepared for the Future
Making Healthy Choices	Comfortable with Others

PREPARED

I have everything I need
with me.

CONNECTED TO MY FAMILY

Being together around
the dinner table with a
meal everyone enjoys
brings us closer.

Aware of My Surroundings	Valued as a Customer	Leading by Example
Finding My Way	Free to Do What I Want	Hopeful for the Future
Comfortable	Stable and Secure	Making Memories
Taken Care Of	Learning New Things	Safe from Harm
Respected as a Person	Providing Opportunities	Improving Myself

3. FEATURES

The next level in the Anatomy of an Experience Framework focuses on how the benefits are delivered. This is the actionable stuff. Features describe the properties or characteristics of a product or service. These are usually pictures of things, in context, with people. They are descriptive of how something works or how you would interact with it.

To think about features, try completing the statement:

IT IS . . .

HEALTHY

My side dish supplements the nutrition that my main dish lacks. It always supports me in balancing my meals.

INTUITIVE

I can use it immediately without a learning curve.

Other ideal feature examples include: IT IS . . .	Easy to Use	Powerful
	Reliable	Helpful
	Smart	Straightforward
	Luxurious	High Quality
	Innovative	Personalized

DURABLE

It should be made with materials that stand the test of time.

WELCOMING

It is a comfortable place where I can relax and spend some time.

Organized	Delightful	Intuitive
Simple	Encouraging	Helpful
Fun	Effortless	Accepting
Secure	Capable	Respectful
Proactive	Seamless	Efficient

4. SENSORY CUES

Sensory cues are the concrete details that engage the senses to embody the features. These are pictures of details. They concretely demonstrate how something looks, or acts.

To think about sensory cues, try completing the statement:

IT . . .

has . . .

SUSPENDED PARTICLES

The formula should have visible elements to indicate that the product has a special efficacy.

has a . . .

CITRUS SMELL

A citrus scent is good for a cleaning product. In addition to being a fresh and sweet smell, it also seems effective.

Other ideal sensory cue examples include: IT . . .		
Clear Packaging	Features Whitespace
Toasted	Chimes
Minty Taste	Worded Simply
Seamless	Step-by-Step Instructions
Interesting Garnishes	Natural Motifs

It is . . .
SCIENTIFIC LOOKING

It lets me know that it will work. It is effective and elicits trust.

It is . . .
LIGHTWEIGHT
BUT STRONG

Any non-essential material is removed or hollowed out.

It is . . .
SHORT &
TO THE POINT

Messages use only a few words in one or two sentences.

Wears a Uniform	Reinforced	Smells Woody
Mix of colors	Thick	Feels Scratchy
Soft	Looks Unique	Floral Scent
Light Scent	Creamy	Shiny
Crunchy	See-Through	Metallic

33

CHAPTER 1 REVIEW

A USER-DRIVEN PERSPECTIVE ON DESIGN THINKING

Define value, aligning teams on what people want. Direct creativity toward solving problems grounded in desired experiences. Prototype in a way that communicates experientially. Measure ideas based upon what people find valuable.

DEFINING VALUE: WHAT PEOPLE REALLY WANT

Utilize a structured process to define value. The rest of this book is built on this approach.

IDEAL EXPERIENCE RESEARCH

Think experientially. Connect the dots between what you make and how it makes people feel.

USING THE PRINCIPLES

ASPIRATIONAL

Aspirations, desires, or what people wish for are the high-level outcomes of the anatomy framework.

HOLISTIC

The Anatomy of Experience framework describes complete experiences and connects them to things in the world.

ACTIONABLE

Sensory cues are concrete.

VISUAL

Different types of
imagery can be used
to describe each of the
four components of the
anatomy framework.

WHAT YOU CAN DO NEXT

Continually practice thinking experientially. Think about products, services, screens, and places that you interact with. Pay attention to how these interactions make you feel. Begin to notice what it is about these things that makes you feel that way.

CHAPTER 2:

Relevant   Aspirational   Holistic   Rigorous   Actionable   Visual

CHOOSING A RESEARCH APPROACH

DEFINE YOUR
RESEARCH OBJECTIVES

As we mentioned in the introduction, your design needs to accomplish a greater goal. Typically this is a business result. In order to design something that delivers a meaningful experience you need to understand a variety of things. This will inevitably lead to questions for which you need to find answers. These questions are the goals for your research.

SELECT A RESEARCH
APPROACH

There are many ways to get the information you need from people.

CONSIDER THE
END DELIVERABLE

You need to think about the type of story you want to tell at the end of your research.

DEFINE YOUR RESEARCH OBJECTIVES

Let's start with how to establish objectives for your research. To achieve your desired outcomes, you need to define what exactly you want to learn from your research. Learning objectives, or key questions, are the questions that you have about the desired user experience, the experience people want to have with what you create. The answers to these questions will help ensure that you deliver a meaningful and enjoyable experience to the user.

EXAMPLE LEARNING OBJECTIVES

Uncover how a financial services app should communicate privacy and security to its users.

Define the desires and pain points of patients receiving a diagnosis for the first time.

Understand how small business owners make decisions about their insurance and finances.

TYPE OF INFORMATION THAT CAN BE ELICITED	DEFINITION	DESIGN APPLICATION
Use Case	The scenarios in which a person engages with something.	You have a clear understanding of the situations you are designing for.
Context	The environment or circumstance of use.	You understand where something will be used/occur and the impact of the surroundings that must be addressed in your solution.
Definitive Moments	The interactions that stand out to a person when using or doing something.	You are aware of the key touchpoints and can ensure that each one is addressed.
Usage Experience	The emotional outcome of interacting with something.	You identify challenges, frustrations, and pain points that can be addressed in your design.
Process	The specific steps a person goes through when using or doing something.	You are able to ensure that your solution flows seamlessly into what is happening without being disruptive.
Attitudes	Beliefs or perceptions about the category.	You are able to conduct your discussion with a person in a way that he or she can relate to.
Motivations	The goals a person has when doing something.	You understand the relevance of what you are designing.
Aspirations	The desired emotional state (the way a person wants to feel) when engaging with something.	This is very similar to motivations. You understand why people want what you are designing. Its value.
Benefits	The expectations a person has when engaging with something.	You understand what your solution needs to accomplish.
Features	The characteristics of a product or service.	You know what to solve for.
Sensory Cues	The way a product or service looks or acts. Its personality.	You know how to deliver your solution.

Based on your learning objectives, you will need to get certain types of information from people. The information you gather might include use cases, context, definitive moments, usage experiences, processes, attitudes, motivations, aspirations, and sought-after benefits, features, and sensory cues.

Each type of information has an actionable impact on what you will design. Remember that for something to be actionable, it needs to provide concrete direction. Actionable information addresses the research objectives and turns them into more understandable, attainable components.

SELECT A RESEARCH APPROACH

In order to get the right kind of information to achieve your objectives, you now need the appropriate research approach. A research approach is the combination of methods you will use to get the information you need from people. Understanding how each type of information can be applied to your design and your deliverable helps you connect your research objectives to your research approach.

Research approaches can be broken down into understanding three elements:*

1. What people say
2. What people do
3. What people make

---

*Sanders, E.B.-N. (1992). "Converging Perspectives: Product Development Research for the 1990s." *Design Management Journal*, Fall.

What people say can be captured through interviews and questionnaires. What people do can be captured through observation and self-documentation. What people make can be captured by giving them tools to express themselves.

There are many types of research approaches. The important thing to remember is that each approach delivers different kinds of information. What are the conversations you want to have with people that will achieve your research objectives? Your research approach and the methods you select will define these conversations, and these conversations will ultimately form the outcomes of your research.

Don't forget that the information you get from people must be actionable. The approach you choose and the conversations you have must help to (1) clearly define the problem you're solving, and (2) identify how your solution needs to be delivered.

An easy way to start thinking about research approaches is to break it down into one of four areas:

	EXPERIENCE	THING TO BE DESIGNED
CURRENT	How does the person feel today when using the product or service?	What about the "thing" is making the person feel that way?
IDEAL	How does the person want to feel when using the product or service?	What does the "thing" need to do to deliver the desired experience?

A research effort can take two avenues: the current experience or the future/ideal experience. Understanding the current experience will yield areas of opportunity. Identifying the ideal experience enables you to understand what people desire and why. While both types of information are valuable, we believe knowledge of the ideal "thing" is the most actionable piece of information you can get from a research study.

OPEN-ENDED ONLINE QUESTIONS

Open-ended online questions capture attitudes and beliefs about the category, elements of context, and steps in a process or journey. These questions might be adapted to cover both current and ideal studies.

Attitudes & Beliefs:

- How do you feel about . . .
- What are your thoughts about . . .
- What do you prefer . . .
- What do you like about . . .
- What do you dislike about . . .

Context:

- Who are the people involved . . .
- What tools do you use . . .
- What information is important . . .
- Where do you . . .

PROCESS MAPPING

Process mapping describes what happens over time in a current experience. It often identifies the steps a person or team goes through, the tools and information they use, and the people they interact with.

SELF-DOCUMENTATION

Self-documentation is effective because it enables people to capture moments of a current experience that are meaningful to them. These moments often occur when the subject matter is personal or does not permit observation, or when the observer might not be present. This approach also allows data capture over several weeks, which is much more cost-effective than multiple observations of the same person.

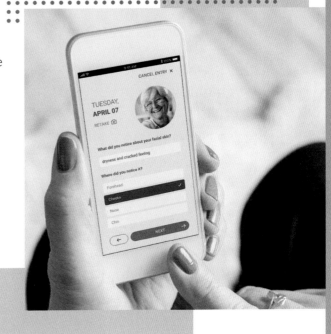

JOURNEY MAPPING

Journey mapping focuses on the definitive moments in a person's experience. It can be used effectively to identify current or ideal interactions.

ETHNOGRAPHY & CONTEXTUAL INQUIRY

Ethnography and contextual inquiry are useful for bringing current situations to life, and understanding context, pain points, journeys, or processes.

EXPERIENCE COLLAGING

Experience collaging brings to life how a current experience feels. This is a very efficient way to identify pain points and context at a holistic level. When combined with ideal experience, collaging (how people want to feel in a specific experience within a given category) can highlight gaps that serve as opportunities for improving the experience.

CO-CREATION OR PARTICIPATORY DESIGN

Co-creation or participatory design uses abstract stimuli that deconstruct an ideal experience. This activity enables people to build the product or service that will deliver their desired experience. It is an effective approach to deliver a concrete understanding of what needs to happen to deliver the ideal solution. This approach can also be applied to process and journey maps when the ideal "thing" would have steps or a process.

TYPE OF INFORMATION THAT CAN BE ELICITED	DEFINITION	DESIGN APPLICATION
Use Case	How a person engages with a product or service to fulfill a goal.	You have a clear understanding of the situations you are designing for.
Context	The environment or circumstance of use.	You understand how and where the product or service will be used and the impact of surroundings on its use.
Definitive Moments	The interactions that stand out to a person when using or doing something.	You are aware of the key moments and can ensure that each one is addressed.
Usage Experience	The emotional outcome of interacting with something.	You identify challenges, frustrations, and pain points that can be addressed in your design.
Process	The specific steps a person goes through when using or doing something.	You are able to ensure that your solution flows seamlessly into what is happening without being disruptive.
Attitudes	Beliefs or perceptions about the category.	You are able to conduct your discussion with a person in a way that he or she can relate to.
Motivations	The goals a person has when doing something.	You understand the relevance of what you are designing.
Aspirations	The desired emotional state (the way a person wants to feel) when engaging with something.	This is very similar to motivations. You understand why people want what you are designing – its value.
Benefits	The expectations a person has when engaging with something.	You understand what your solution needs to accomplish.
Features	The characteristics of a product or service.	You know what to solve for.
Sensory Cues	The way a product or service looks or acts. Its personality.	You know how to deliver your solution.

RESEARCH METHODS

Self-documentation, contextual inquiry

Self-documentation, contextual inquiry, experience collaging

Self-documentation, contextual inquiry, journey mapping

Self-documentation, contextual inquiry, experience collaging

Self-documentation, contextual inquiry, process mapping

Open-ended online questions, interviewing

Open-ended online questions, interviewing

Open-ended online questions, interviewing, experience collaging

Interviewing, experience collaging

Interviewing, co-creation stimulus kit

Co-creation stimulus kit

The best research approach is typically a combination of methods. For example, an approach that uses self-documentation + experience collaging + co-creation provides context, an understanding of pain points and aspirations, and clear direction on what to make.

No matter what approach is chosen, it is key that the approach must answer your learning objectives in an actionable way. This chart shows how different types of information can be applied, and which methods can be used to attain that information.

Once your research is complete, you will need to tell the story of what you learned. We will review this in more detail during our discussion on Insight Translation in chapter 10.

CONSIDER THE END DELIVERABLE

Along with thinking about your learning objectives and how to address them, you will need to consider your deliverable in your up-front decision making. The deliverable is how you will share research findings and tell your story. We will spend more time talking about the importance of story in chapter 10, Telling the Story of the Future. For now, it is important to have this end result in mind as you start your research. To some extent, your research objectives point you toward your deliverable. Here are some common types of deliverables to familiarize yourself with.

What do you dislike about y

Why did you get into this line of work?

What makes a good police officer?

How would you describe yourself (professiona sonally)?

doing when you're not at work

PERSONAS

Personas bring the "who" (your target audience or user types) to life. A good persona makes it clear why they want what they want and what you need to make for them. They should stem naturally from the research and not feel contrived.

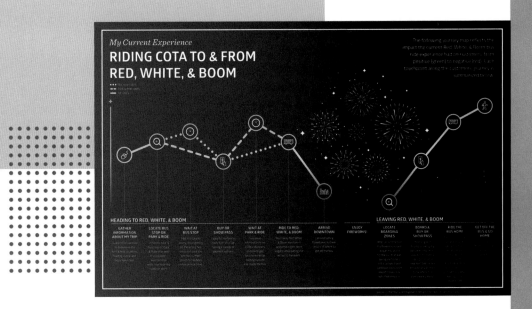

CURRENT JOURNEY MAPS

Journey maps describe what happens over time and are based on the experience of today. These are focused on the definitive moments in the mind of the user as opposed to the steps or procedures people go through.

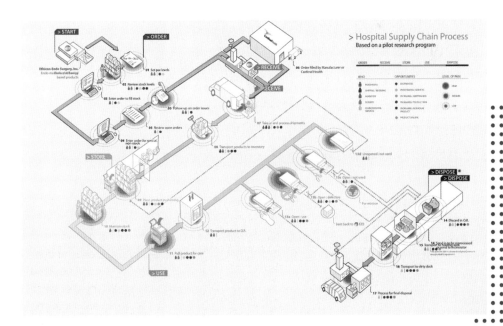

PROCEDURE OR PROCESS MAPS

Procedure or process maps describe the steps in a process.

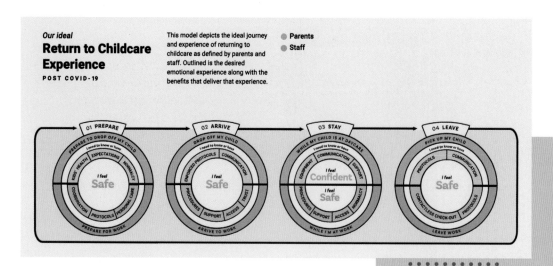

IDEAL JOURNEY MAPS

Ideal journey maps bring to life the experience people want to have over time. The key moments in ideal journey maps tend to be different from the journeys of today. The journey usually starts sooner and ends later than most companies imagine.

The following table shows the kind of information you need for each deliverable:

TYPE OF INFORMATION THAT CAN BE ELICITED	PERSONAS	PROCEDURE OR PROCESS MAPS	CURRENT JOURNEY MAPS
Use Case	X	X	
Context	X	X	X
Definitive Moments			X
Usage Experience	X	X	X
Process	X	X	
Attitudes	X		
Motivations	X	X	X
Aspirations	X		
Benefits	X		
Features	X		
Sensory Cues			

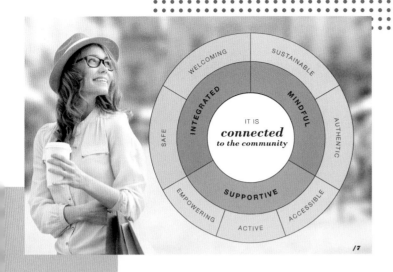

DESIRED EXPERIENCE MODELS

Desired experiences describe the key emotions and benefits of the experience people want to have, often visualized in a framework. Identifying the desired experience means you have identified what the solution ultimately needs to accomplish.

SENSORY CUE FRAMEWORKS

Sensory cue frameworks provide design direction based on user expectations of how a product or service should look, act, and feel.

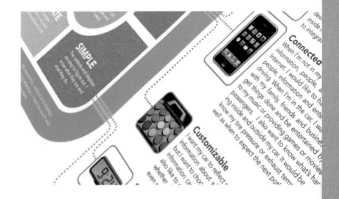

IDEAL JOURNEY MAPS	DESIRED EXPERIENCE MODELS	SENSORY CUE FRAMEWORKS
X		X
X	X	
X		
	X	
X	X	
X	X	X
X	X	X
	X	X
		X

CHAPTER 2 REVIEW

DEFINE YOUR RESEARCH OBJECTIVES

It is important to think about the kind of information you need in order to answer your research questions. There are many types of information your research can generate.

SELECT A RESEARCH APPROACH

Each research approach generates specific types of information. Your research methodology choices need to produce the answers to your research questions.

CONSIDER THE END DELIVERABLE

The methodology choices you make impact the types of deliverables you can create. Once your research is over, you are stuck with the information you garnered. Make sure you have what you need for the type of deliverable you plan to create.

USING THE PRINCIPLES

RELEVANT

Research outputs should connect to the greater goal that your design needs to accomplish.

VISUAL

You want to plan for deliverables that people want to pick up and read.

WHAT YOU CAN DO NEXT

Whenever you think about something you would like to design, start by listing the questions that you have for users and potential users. Make a list of those questions.

CHAPTER 3:

Relevant   Aspirational   Holistic   **Rigorous**   Actionable   Visual

FINDING YOUR TARGET USER

IDENTIFY PARTICIPATION CRITERIA

You need to make sure that you study the kind of people that will actually use what you design (aka your target audience). Your research needs to be credible in order for other people to believe your conclusions. If you study the right people, it will ultimately help you justify your design decisions.

CREATE A SCREENER

You want to create a tool that helps you determine if someone is part of your target audience and a good research participant. If people are familiar with what you are designing, they will be able to share their past experiences and aspirations. This will ensure you get useful information.

FIND YOUR PARTICIPANTS

You need to come up with a plan to discover the people who are right for your study.

IDENTIFY PARTICIPATION CRITERIA

First, you need to identify the criteria for participation in your study. There are a few common areas to consider when defining the kind of people you want to study.

DEMOGRAPHICS

Demographics include data such as age, sex, ethnicity, income, household composition, education, and profession. It is important to make sure you have a broad mix represented in your study so that you get a variety of perspectives.

CATEGORY ENGAGEMENT

Category engagement considers whether people actually buy and use what you want to study. When people are engaged in the category, they have relevant experiences to share with you.

ATTITUDE OR MINDSET

Attitude or mindset is how people think and feel about the category. If you are studying shoes, the opinions of "sneakerheads" would be different from those of people who look for the best deal. Many companies have segments – groups of people based on common characteristics. For example, segments for an oral care brand might include (1) people who care more about having white teeth and (2) people who care more about having a healthy mouth. It's important to consider what attitudes you might be focusing on for your study.

ARTICULATION

Articulation is someone's ability to explain themselves. Checking for articulation ensures that your participants can answer your questions effectively. You can check someone's articulation by asking them to describe something. If their answer is articulate, you will be able to envision what they are describing. For example, you might ask them to describe their favorite food without saying what it is. An articulate answer has evocative adjectives or emotions, like "my favorite food has vibrant green leaves drenched in vinegar, with fresh fruit that is bursting with flavor."

CREATE A SCREENER

These considerations are brought together in what is called a screener. A screener is a series of questions that ensure a person is right for your particular study. Each question in your screener should be designed to either eliminate potential participants from consideration or to proceed to the next question.

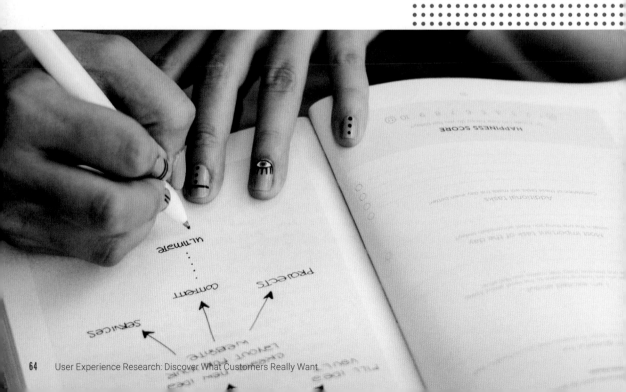

To begin writing your screener, think about the kind of people you want to study. Make a list that describes them in terms of demographics, attitude, and category engagement. Be sure to focus on making your group as diverse as possible. The broader your audience, the larger the market is for your design.

Once you have described the kind of people you do want in your study, think about who you do not want to be involved. These people are called exclusions. The reason for excluding particular people is to eliminate bias. For example, if you are studying shoes, you do not want a person that designs shoes or works in a shoe store because they are too involved in the category. Exclusions are typically the first questions you ask in a screener so you can eliminate them early on. Therefore, be intentional with the overall sequencing of your questions. Think of each question as a filter, starting broad and then narrowing down to segment participants as necessary.

Most of the time, your screener questions should be closed-ended or provide response options. This makes it easier to capture their information and determine who you want to be involved in your study.

Whether you decide to use a formal screener or choose another method to assess potential participants, you always need to explain what you are doing, ask questions to ensure they are the right people, invite them to participate in your study, and then schedule a time and place for their participation.

You can think of a screener as a script for your conversation with a potential participant. An example of what is included in a typical screener is provided on the following page.

We are a team of researchers studying shopping habits to understand the ideal shopping experience. We are looking for shoppers interested in participating in an interview.

Recruit Criteria

Recruiting for 10 participants who are local residents. Participants will be separated into two segments: Power Shopper (makes three or more shopping trips per week), and Weekend Warrior (makes two or less shopping trips per week)

- Mix of 50% Power Shoppers and 50% Weekend Warriors
- Mix of gender and ethnicity
- Are not employed in marketing or research industries
- Must pass criteria on the following pages

Do you use any of the following digital wallets?

___ Apple Wallet
___ Google Pay
___ Apple Pay
___ Android Pay
___ Other (record)
___ I don't use a digital wallet (thank and terminate)

Which of the following best describes your age? (Recruit a mix)

___ Under 25 (thank and terminate)
___ 25 – 34 (minimum 5)
___ 35 – 44
___ 45 – 54
___ 55 – 65
___ 66 or older (thank and terminate)

I tend to think and talk about theories and conjectures, dreams and philosophies, beliefs and fantasies – all the why's and if's of life.

___ I strongly identify with this statement
___ I somewhat identify with this statement
___ I do not identify with this statement

We would like to invite you to participate in a 60-minute interview to learn more about your shopping habits.

The interview will take place at 123 Lolly St, Somewhere, USA. The date and time of your interview will be emailed to you shortly. We ask that you please arrive 5 minutes early to the interview location to allow time for parking and sign-in. Audio and video will be recorded for all sessions and will be used for internal research purposes only. You will be compensated X amount for your completed interview.

Please reach out to email@address.com with any questions or concerns. Thank you, and we look forward to speaking with you!

INTRODUCTION

Explains why you are talking to the potential participant.

CRITERIA OVERVIEW

For research team use only: A breakdown of how many participants you're recruiting (in general, recruit at least 10–12 people per study), segmentation, and the overall demographic criteria that they should meet.

SCREENING QUESTIONS

These are focused on demographics, category engagement, attitude, and/or articulation.

EXCLUSION QUESTIONS

These eliminate undesirable participants from the study.

O
O *Tip: Asking exclusion questions early on makes sure you aren't wasting time getting information from someone you ultimately won't include in your study.*

INVITATION

A request to participate to those who passed the screening questions with a statement of how they will be compensated.

INTERVIEW DETAILS

When and where the interview will take place along with any next steps.

FIND YOUR PARTICIPANTS

Once you have a screener, it's time to recruit. Keep in mind, the more specific your screening criteria are, the harder it will be to find the right people. However, there are many ways to get creative with approaching your recruit.

If your research project has a dedicated budget, you might hire a market research recruiter to find participants for your study. Hiring a recruiter will require you to have a detailed screener. Regardless of whether you use a third-party recruiter or do it yourself, having a screener will greatly assist you in your recruiting efforts. You will also want to come up with a way to capture participants' screener responses, which is helpful when it comes to (1) making sure you're following your recruit guidelines, (2) analyzing the data from your study, and (3) telling the story of your research.

For this version of the book, we leave it up to you to get creative about how you find the right people. Try using social media, standing outside a store that sells what you want to study, going to the park, or looking for friends of friends. Get creative and have fun!

CHAPTER 3 REVIEW

IDENTIFY PARTICIPATION CRITERIA

You never want to design anything without a target audience in mind. The key factors to consider when describing your target audience are demographics, category engagement, attitude or mindset, and articulation.

CREATE A SCREENER

A screener is a commonly used tool. Developing a strong screener helps establish your credibility with other research disciplines such as market research or consumer insights.

FIND YOUR PARTICIPANTS

Your research is only as good as the people you study. These people will serve as the foundation for your design decisions. Make sure you have a solid plan for locating them.

USING THE PRINCIPLES

RELEVANT

You want to study the people that will actually buy and use what you design.

RIGOROUS

If you study the wrong people, you run the risk of designing the wrong thing. The people you study are the foundation of your research.

WHAT YOU CAN DO NEXT

Know who you are designing for. Outline your target user.
Make sure these people exist.

CHAPTER 4:

Relevant   Aspirational   Holistic   Rigorous   Actionable   Visual

HAVING EFFECTIVE CONVERSATIONS

FORMULATE YOUR QUESTIONS

The questions you ask a research participant should be directly related to your research objectives. You are going from a few big objectives to a detailed set of questions.

CREATE A DISCUSSION GUIDE

You want to have a structured plan for how you do your interviews. This tool puts all of your interview questions in a structure that flows.

CONDUCT INTERVIEWS

Moderation, or guiding a discussion, is a skill that you develop over the course of many conversations. Everyone has their own unique approach, and it takes a lot of practice to discover your own method that is not only effective at getting the data you need but also authentic to who you are.

FORMULATE YOUR QUESTIONS

In order to formulate your discussion questions, you will need to start with your research objectives (see chapter 2). These objectives tend to be very big questions that are likely full of many smaller, specific questions. You can start by thinking through these smaller questions and how you would phrase them to a participant. Since this is generative research, you will want to ask open-ended questions. This allows the participant to talk openly about what they think is important without being biased by the question.

Depending on the answers you receive, you may want to follow up with a list of probes that you've prepared in advance. A probe is a follow-up question that dives deeper into a participant's response to get more detail. When and how to use probes will be discussed further later in this chapter.

TYPES OF QUESTIONS

Here is a framework for helping you think through your questions using an example of automotive entertainment. The rows are various levels of granularity, or detail, pertaining to the category. The columns are elements from the Anatomy of an Ideal Experience Framework: emotions, subject (the product/service), context, and actions (behaviors, routines, processes, activities).

	EMOTIONS	THE PRODUCT OR SERVICE	CONTEXT	ACTIONS
TRANSPORTATION				
CARS				
CAR INTERIOR				
ENTERTAINMENT SYSTEM				
PREFERENCES				
THE CLOCK				
THE CLOCK CONTROLS				

Each empty box in this matrix represents a different conversation you will be having with someone. It's important to know ahead of time which conversations you want to have so that you can be intentional in the interview. This allows you to be efficient with your research so that you can get the information you need.

You can think about these rows, or levels of granularity, like zooming in and out of a map. At a high level you might be looking at transportation as a general industry, then you can zoom in to a category such as cars, and then zoom further into specific components. Based upon the type of conversation you want to have, you might want to zoom out a little to help the participant step into the discussion. This gradual introduction from a high-level to a more narrow topic gives participants context and allows them to form their own understanding of the subject. Take care not to zoom out so far that you waste time getting to the subject of your discussion.

AVOIDING BIAS IN YOUR QUESTIONS

The way you word your questions is extremely important. It is easy to fall into the trap of asking leading questions (e.g., "Wouldn't you like to have a better clock?") Remember, you want to ask open-ended questions.

Here are some other ways to think about asking open-ended questions without bias:

GENERAL QUESTIONS

- Tell me what you know about ____
- Show me how you ____ (elaborate on completed artifacts)
- Tell me about the last time you ____ (past experience)
- What are you doing now? (more detail in the moment)

UNDERSTANDING ATTITUDE, MOTIVATION, OR GOALS

- What motivated you to ____? (understand motivation/goals)
- Help me understand your thought process when ____? (understand motivation/goals)
- What did you consider or reject when thinking about ____? (understand motivation/goals)
- What popped into your head when you heard/thought about/saw ____? (understand attitude/motivation/goals)
- What are your thoughts about ____?
- What's important to ____?

Here are some ways to think about asking follow-up probing questions:

GENERAL PROBES

- For what reasons? What else?
- How would you describe that feeling/ thought in different words?
- Tell me more about that _____
- What do you mean by _____?
- How does that differ from _____?
- In what situations do you _____?
- How is that similar to (or different) from _____?
- What prompted/motivated you to _____?
- What did you take into consideration when thinking about _____?
- Help me understand your thought process . . .
- What factors got you to this point?

EMOTIONAL PROBES

- How would that make you feel?

BENEFIT PROBES

- What would you need to feel that way?
- What would the impact of that be?

FEATURE PROBES

- What should it be like to provide that?
- What should it do?
- What does that signal to you?

ATTRIBUTE PROBES

- How would you know it is?
- What does that look, sound, feel, smell, or interact like?

CREATE A DISCUSSION GUIDE

As we have pointed out, there are many different research methods. Each method will require a different set of discussion questions. Regardless of the method, you will need a discussion guide. A discussion guide is a tool to remain intentional and think through the structure and flow of the interview, as well as the timing for each question or section of the guide. Ultimately, you want to use the discussion guide as a checklist and conduct interviews in a way that is natural and conversational. A discussion guide should never be used like a script. However, at the same time you need to execute your interviews in a consistent way so that you can find patterns. A discussion guide represents your plan for a repeatable process.

Discussion guides are typically broken into sections that help you navigate an interview. Each section is usually allocated a certain amount of time, and questions are sequenced to help participants relate to the subject. Your discussion's structure needs to make it easy for the participant to step into the mindset required to answer the questions. There are many ways to sequence your questions. However you decide to do so, it's important to organize questions efficiently to focus on information relevant to the study.

On the following page, you'll find an example discussion guide for your reference.

Introduction (5 minutes)

Hello! Thank you for taking the time to speak with us. My name is _____ and I'll be guiding our discussion. This is my partner, who will be taking notes and making sure we cover everything.

Over the next hour, we're going to be talking about your experience with your vehicle's entertainment features. There are a couple things I'd like to cover before we get started.

- We are independent researchers, and there are no right or wrong answers. We're interested in your honest experience.
- Please sign this form to acknowledge we will be recording this interview, and everything we discuss today will be confidential.
- Please feel free to ask questions or bring up any other thoughts or suggestions you might have.
- Lastly, we have a lot of material to cover today. At times I might ask you to go into more detail, and at other times I might interrupt to move on. Please don't be offended; this is to respect your time and ensure we cover everything.

Contextual Questions (30 minutes)

1. Where do you typically go in your car?
2. Who is with you?
3. In moments like this, how do you use your entertainment system?
4. Who else uses your system?
5. What is important in an entertainment system?
6. What are your thoughts on the way you set your preferences?
7. Have you ever changed the clock?
8. Have you noticed anything about changing the clock?
9. What is important when changing the clock?

Experiential Questions (30 minutes)

1. How do you feel when using your entertainment system?
2. What causes you to feel this way?
3. How did changing the clock make you feel?
4. What about changing the clock made you feel this way?

Wrap-Up (10 minutes)

Those are all the questions I have for you today. Let me check with our note-taker to make sure we covered everything. In the meantime, do you have any final thoughts or questions for us? Thank you again for your time!

INTRODUCTION

An effective introduction sets up the study and accomplishes several tasks:

- Introduces the research team
- Outlines the topic of discussion
- Requests the signing of a consent form
- Mentions any recording, such as audio, video, or photography
- States how long the research session will take
- Sets participant expectations

SEQUENCED QUESTIONS

Questions are organized to start broadly and then narrow in to be more specific. This enables the participant to relate to what you are studying in a way that is meaningful to them.

Another helpful way to structure conversations is by sequencing questions to follow the Anatomy of an Ideal Experience.

WRAP-UP

Thank participants once again and offer any closing remarks. This provides the note-taker with a final opportunity to ask questions that might have been missed. It also gives participants a chance to share any other thoughts or ask any questions they might have.

> **Tip:** Writing verbatim questions helps you organize and articulate your thoughts, but it is not necessary to follow these exactly – an interview guide is not meant to be a script but a checklist to ensure you have covered all of the topics of discussion.

CONDUCT INTERVIEWS

Your discussion guide tells you what questions to ask, but it doesn't tell you how to ask them. Interviewing is much easier when you put people at ease and inspire them to share with you.

While moderating, you should always be aware of the situation and be able to quickly change strategies to get the data you need. By keeping the interview focused and guiding the participant to stay on track, you will be able to stay in control of the interview without leading or alienating the participant.

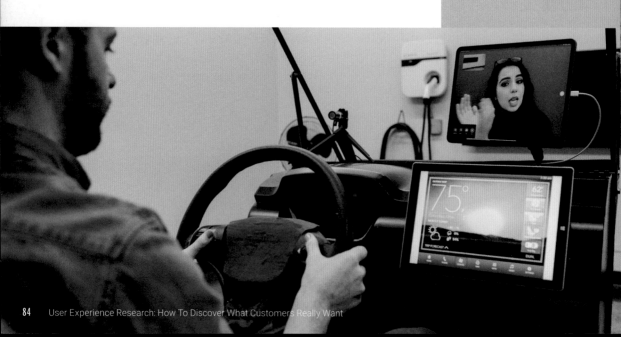

MAKE THEM FEEL COMFORTABLE

Inspiring participants to share their experiences begins with making them feel at ease. Here are some points to keep in mind when conducting your interviews.

SET AND MEET EXPECTATIONS

Introduce research team members, inform participants of the purpose of the interview, and set expectations regarding activities, compensation, and time.

RESPECT THEIR PRIVACY

Show respect for the participant's privacy by assuring them of confidentiality and request permission to photograph or record the session.

ESTABLISH RAPPORT

Take time at the beginning to break the ice by asking general questions that will be easy for the participant to answer. This will put them at ease and demonstrate that you want to have a conversation, not just an interview.

ACTIVELY LISTEN

Convey genuine interest verbally and non-verbally: lean forward, mirror their posture and language, and maintain eye contact.

REPEAT BACK TO CONFIRM

Repeating statements might seem simple, but participants find it reassuring because it confirms that you understood them correctly. Be sure the person knows that he or she should correct you if you are wrong.

WATCH BODY LANGUAGE

Gauge how your participant is feeling and be aware of non-verbal cues to know how to proceed. Watch body language. For example, expressive gestures (like talking with your hands) might indicate your participant is engaged, while a lack could indicate boredom or fatigue.

IT'S ALL ABOUT THEM

Remind participants that they should only consider how they would like things to be, not how other people (older/younger, more/less tech savvy) might. Because you'll talk to many other people during the research, they are only responsible for representing themselves.

Tip: *If your participant begins to display signs of fatigue, that's your signal to offer a break, or prioritize and reorder your questions to make sure key topics are covered.*

STICK TO YOUR PLAN, BUT BE FLEXIBLE

Although creating your discussion guide, probes, and sequencing has given you a plan, be prepared to go off-script. This is why we encourage discussion guides to be treated as just that. Every participant is different, and some will require you to adjust your strategy to get the information you need.

DIG DEEP FOR HIDDEN MEANING

Look for the underlying meaning of words to uncover deeper associations and motivations. Have them explain the obvious, such as what "easy" means to them, or why "easy" is important in this context. Non-verbal cues will also give you signs on when to stop probing and move on to the next topic to avoid irritating your participant. Be sensitive to what they are capable of describing.

KNOW YOUR NEXT MOVE

Be present and in the moment, but also know your next move. Getting to your goal will require thinking several moves ahead. Processing what the participant is saying, if it applies to the project objectives, and what you still need to get in order to meet all of your objectives will allow you to keep the flow of the interview going and anticipate what question you should ask next.

ADAPT TO THE SITUATION

Be creative and find alternative ways to get the data if your proposed method or question isn't working.

KNOW YOUR STUDY

A deep understanding of what information you need to obtain will allow you to be flexible in how you get it during the interview. Adapt your communication style to fit the participant. For example, try asking for specific examples if a participant is unable to answer abstract questions.

TAKE REMINDER NOTES

Understand each important "why" behind what they tell you. In a fast-paced interview, it can be difficult to remember what you need to follow up on. Rather than relying on memory, take moderator notes. Write down a word or short phrase to jog your memory, so that you can follow up on specific points or choose to move on to another topic.

STAY IN SCOPE

Know enough about your objectives to understand what's important, and what's in scope based on project goals. Ensure questions and follow-ups are focused. Don't go outside of your project scope by trying to solve their problems, or turning the conversation to you or your company. Your goal is to understand their experiences and thoughts.

LADDER UP OR DRILL DOWN TO THE RIGHT LEVEL

Know where you are and where you need to go. You can use a technique called "laddering" to get information at a specific level of the participant's experience. For example, if your participant focuses on what they do or want, you might need to ask "why" multiple times in order to understand the "why" behind it. Using the previously mentioned discussion guide framework, you can drill down or ladder up.

AVOID BIAS IN YOUR CONVERSATION

Good moderating means that your participants are doing most of the talking. Remember that you're interviewing them to understand their thoughts and experience, not to prove a point. Use these tips to avoid biasing your participants' responses.

ESTABLISH YOUR NEUTRALITY

Make sure your participant knows that your role is neutral, there are no wrong answers, and they shouldn't worry about offending you because you aren't the designer — even if you are. Ensure that you don't interject your own opinions, always answer questions with a question, and be aware and maintain control of your verbal and non-verbal responses. If you show excitement about a particular response, that could introduce bias by leading the person to believe there's a particular response you'd like to hear. This might cause the interviewee to become reluctant to express everything they think. Start with general, open-ended questions, working toward specific questions.

PROMOTE THEIR EXPERTISE

Maintain a genuinely respectful tone and encourage them to enlighten you — never correct the interviewee. Be aware of the tone and wording of questions to avoid sounding judgmental or accusatory. For example, if a participant seems to contradict themselves, ask them to resolve it by saying, "Earlier, I thought I heard ___, but just now I thought you said ___. I'm confused. Help me understand."

ASK OPEN-ENDED QUESTIONS

Ask open-ended, not yes/no questions. After their answer, pause to allow the person to add any last thoughts. Follow up with open-ended probes to fully understand what the participant means, but watch your tone and wording to avoid making the participant uncomfortable and turning the interview into an interrogation.

GUIDE, DON'T LEAD

Word questions clearly and directly without leading your participant. Asking a general question like "How did that go?" Isn't specific enough to keep on track, but being overly specific could be leading. Ask a question that's open, but gives enough direction like "Will you walk me through your thought process?" to let them know the types of things you're interested in, without leading them to an answer.

STAY ON TIME

Once you've set expectations, meet them. A deep understanding of your discussion guide and research objectives will help you navigate the interview and adhere to any constraints.

RESPECT THEIR TIME

Let the participant know that you might have to interrupt them occasionally to move the interview forward out of consideration for their time and be sure to start and end interviews on time.

WATCH THE TIME

Mind the clock. Structure the conversation and make a plan to manage time effectively. Having time checkpoints in mind for sections of your discussion guide will help you know if you need to speed up or if you can slow down and get more detail.

KNOW WHEN TO MOVE ON

Redirect non-productive conversations, and don't allow participants to venture too far off topic. For example, "That's an interesting story, but in the interest of time, I want to get your thoughts on the next topic."

As you develop your personal moderating style, you'll find techniques that do, and don't, work for you. To get you started, here are some good habits to cultivate, and some bad ones to avoid.

DO	DON'T
Speak at a good volume	Talk as much or more than participants
Be comfortable with silence – let them think	Ask more than one question at a time
Vary the style of asking questions	Miss a chance to probe on something important
Ask open-ended questions	Use the same opening (why . . .) repeatedly
Ask short questions to get long answers	Ask yes/no questions
Ask direct questions	Help participants answer questions
Probe for clarity	Discuss your opinions
Show unconditional positive regard	Give a possible answer in a question
Be specific when giving instructions	Respond with words that imply judgment
Demonstrate understanding (e.g., "I hear you," "I see," "Hmm")	
Use participants' words to probe further	

CHAPTER 4 REVIEW

FORMULATE YOUR QUESTIONS

Make sure that your questions align with your research objectives. Be intentional with your questions. Know where you want to go with the discussion and have a plan. Stick with open-ended questions. Don't bias people by providing your own answer to the question.

CREATE A DISCUSSION GUIDE

Use this tool to structure your interview. Make sure your questions have a logical flow that is easy for your participants to follow. Timing is critical, so make sure you address it in your guide. This plan enables you to have a repeatable process, so that later on you can find patterns in your data.

CONDUCT INTERVIEWS

Make people feel comfortable. A discussion guide is a plan, not a script, so keep your research objectives in mind as you conduct interviews. Be flexible but consistent in your discussions. Don't bias people. Bring a clock so you can stay on time. Be yourself.

USING THE PRINCIPLES

RELEVANT

The questions you ask must connect to your research objectives. Be intentional.

RIGOROUS

It's easy to "lead the witness." Don't conduct interviews in a way that creates bias. You want to get to the truth.

WHAT YOU CAN DO NEXT

Train yourself to naturally ask open-ended questions and probing questions. Try practicing using open-ended questions in your daily life and focus on letting others lead you to the next question. Watch people conduct interviews on news and talk shows. Decide if the questions being asked are done in an open-ended way or a leading way.

CAPTURING CLEAR DATA

STRUCTURE YOUR DATA

When you execute your research approach, you will generate data. It's important to have a plan for how you will capture and organize it.

USE A SPREADSHEET TOOL

Spreadsheet software, such as Microsoft Excel or Google Sheets, is a critical tool for design research.

TAKE GOOD NOTES

Once your research fielding is complete, this is what you will be using to tell your story.

STRUCTURE YOUR DATA

The information you generate from your research is called data.

After you have conducted your research, your data is what you will use to draw conclusions and tell your story.

You will need to create a framework for capturing and managing your data.

In chapter 9 we will be studying analysis. This is where you use your data to draw conclusions. A data structure makes this go much faster. This framework also ensures that when multiple people are capturing data, they are doing it the same way.

The following page shows an example of a data template we typically use.

> **Tip:** *Creating structure with columns will allow you to sort or filter to see only the information you need and compare responses across interviews or participants for faster analysis.*

NOTE ID NUMBER

Records the order the notes were taken. This allows you to refer to the original order once you start organizing them.

PARTICIPANT ID

Is typically a letter and number combination that records which person the note came from. This is important for doing frequency counts (something we will discuss more in chapter 9).

TOPIC OR QUESTION

Records what prompted the comment. This adds context and allows you to sort the data and see all the responses to a given question.

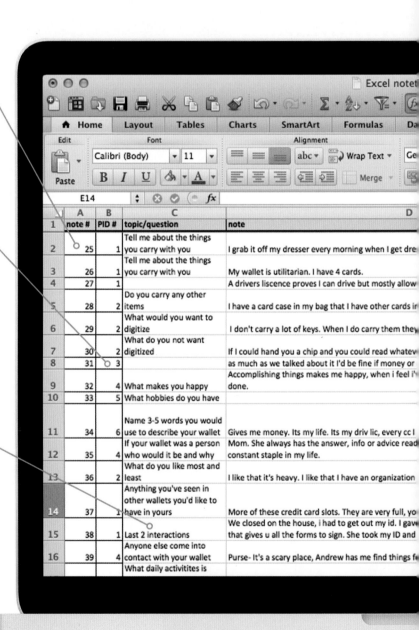

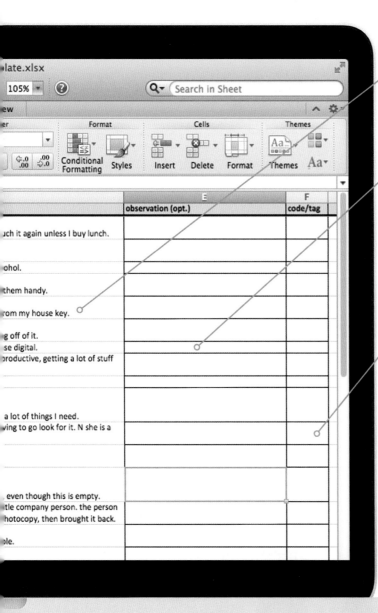

NOTE

Records any comments made by the participant.

OBSERVATION

Depending on the study's goals, you might want to include observations in your notes. This optional step is used to record things noticed by the researchers or to add context.

CODE OR TAG

A word or short phrase that organizes your data into similar stories or ideas. This will allow you to filter your notes. It can be used in the field or afterward during analysis.

CAPTURING DATA

There are several ways to capture data.
Each has advantages and disadvantages.

PEN & PAPER

A note-taking template can be as simple as labeled sections on a page. Taking notes by hand provides portability when in contextual environments. It also provides more flexibility to layer drawings or make connections. This approach takes more time because you have to enter the data into your template later.

LAPTOP

Using a computer to enter notes directly into a structured template eliminates data entry later and saves a step. However, depending upon the context, a computer might be cumbersome or obtrusive.

TRANSCRIPTS

You can record audio and video during an interview. There are apps you can download to record your conversations. Recording is very portable and convenient when in the field. If you don't have a note-taker, this approach allows you to focus on the interview vs. also having to capture data.

There are a lot of digital tools that can transcribe audio recordings. When doing socially distanced interviews on Zoom, transcripts are automatically provided. Even after your interview is transcribed, you still need to enter your data into the template. It is also possible to listen to the recording later and input the data.

All of these approaches will work. It really depends on the context and subject matter of your interview.

Ultimately, the data structure can be used as a note-taking tool or for inputting data at a later time.

USE A SPREADSHEET TOOL

While studying design you have learned many new software programs. Spreadsheet software is a critical tool for design research. Once you begin analysis and synthesis, covered in chapter 9, you will need to use this tool. To structure your data, you will need to learn how to use either Microsoft Excel or Google Sheets.

If you review the Google Sheets tutorial prepared by Google, you will encounter a variety of features and tips. Reviewing this training will ensure you can handle all data-related tasks. Microsoft offers a variety of video trainings and templates to help you acclimate to Excel and streamline your processes.

Whatever solution you use, it's a good idea to know how the software works, learn about data sorting, and discover how to do simple formulas for counts and percentages.

TAKE GOOD NOTES

We typically have one person moderate and one person document the conversation by taking notes.

It's important that what happens in your research gets documented. You need an accurate account of what your research participant said, did, and made.

The information that lives in a single cell in the note section of your template is very important. Knowing the difference between a good note and a bad note will ensure that you don't have gaps in your data capture.

FIVE PRINCIPLES OF GOOD NOTE-TAKING

1. BE COMPLETE

Each note must stand on its own. Include context so the note is not ambiguous and doesn't rely on previous notes to make sense. To do so, add clarifying statements in brackets. For example, "That [large graphic] would be perfect for me." The brackets will allow you to later differentiate any additions from what a participant said.

Similarly, call out observations in order to clarify and add context that would otherwise be lost. For example, "That [large graphic] would be perfect for me [participant too short to see smaller graphic]."

Make sure to capture both the "what" and "why" to avoid holes in your data. For example, the note "The [large graphic] would be perfect for me" has a "what," but the "why" is missing. If the note is missing the "why," make sure to probe for clarification.

2. BE DISCRETE

Each individual note should represent one distinct thought, theme, or idea. Doing this will aid in your analysis later. Having a large paragraph with many ideas can be tedious when you're analyzing.

Keep the context when splitting notes that contain multiple ideas. For example, "The color of the screen is soothing. I also like the icon in the corner because it is easy to understand." It should be split into two notes: "The color of the screen is soothing," and "I like the icon in the corner [of the screen] because it is easy to understand."

3. STAY RELEVANT

Keep research goals in mind to gauge the relevance of what a participant says. You want to ensure you're capturing the level of detail needed to make the notes usable in analysis without adding unnecessary detail. For example, recording that the participant uses software is more important than the exact name of the software. However, if you're unsure if a note is in or out of scope, write it down. Taking down unnecessary detail might slow you down and create extra data to sort through, but not getting enough detail might make the note useless during analysis.

4. DON'T JUDGE

Don't judge the information. If you're analyzing and judging the data while trying to capture it, you could miss or leave information out because you decided it wasn't important. Additionally, you might fall behind the active discussion while you're busy assessing a previous statement. Include notes that provide context even if they don't contribute directly to answering a question. This related data can help to build a fuller understanding of the ecosystem of your topic and might reveal useful information in analysis.

5. AVOID BIAS

It's critical that you focus on capturing what people actually say. You don't want to document what you think you are hearing or only what you think is important or interesting. Striving to take verbatim notes will avoid misrepresenting participants and biasing your data.

CHAPTER 5 REVIEW

STRUCTURE YOUR DATA

Have a plan for how you will capture and organize your data.

USE A SPREADSHEET TOOL

Don't wait to do this. Your ability to analyze and synthesize your data later on will depend on it.

TAKE GOOD NOTES

A good note is complete, discrete, relevant, non-judgmental, and unbiased.

USING THE PRINCIPLES

RIGOROUS

This is a data-driven process. You don't want to ground your design in inaccurate data. Notes must accurately reflect what occurred in your research.

WHAT YOU CAN DO NEXT

Become familiar with Microsoft Excel or Google Sheets. Take some tutorials. Start noticing the notes you take in class. Practice making your notes complete, discrete, relevant, and unbiased. Think about what probes could be asked to create a more complete note. Work with the moderator to ensure your research sessions will yield the information you need.

CHAPTER 6:

Relevant   Aspirational   Holistic   Rigorous   Actionable   Visual

DESCRIBING EXPERIENCES WITH STIMULI

UNDERSTAND THE APPLICATIONS OF COLLAGING

This tool can capture many different types of information.

PREPARE COLLAGE EXERCISES

A collage activity is comprised of a canvas and stimuli.

CONDUCT COLLAGE EXERCISES

You need to know how to present these activities to people and how to moderate the explanation of what participants have created.

UNDERSTAND THE APPLICATIONS OF COLLAGING

This is a research approach we use quite often. It goes by many names: collaging, co-creation, participatory design, and projective techniques. The idea is to give people things (stimuli) like pictures and words, and have them use these to describe something. This approach can be done in many different ways to meet a variety of research objectives.

Projective exercises are built using a canvas, words, images, and sometimes objects, smells, sounds, and screen animations (multisensory stimuli). People choose the items that are meaningful to them and place them on the canvas in the appropriate area.

Once people select the stimuli, they describe what the selected items mean in relation to the area of focus.

We are going to focus on types of exercises that we use the most.

EXPERIENCE COLLAGING

Understanding current experiences: situations

Collaging can be used to get a holistic view of situations. When used in this manner the approach delivers an emotional perspective that describes what is happening and the emotional outcome the situation has on the user.

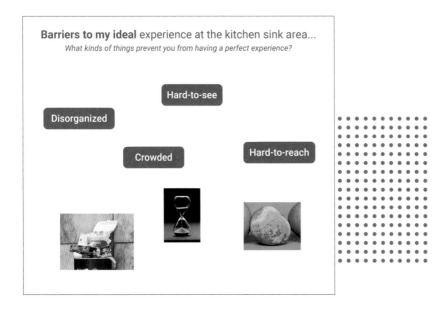

Understanding desired experiences: situational outcomes

Used to discover desired benefits that users seek from a product or service along with the emotional state people are seeking.

SENSORY CUE COLLAGING

Defining how people want benefits delivered in context

As stated in chapter 2, sensory cues describe the personality of a product or service: how it looks, acts, or feels at the sensory level. This information tends to be very concrete and actionable for many functions, e.g., Design, Engineering, Marketing.

It is easiest to think about these approaches in relation to the anatomy of an ideal experience:
1) approaches that describe an experience within the context of a situation (I feel).
2. approaches that describe the "thing" (product or service) that delivers the desired experience in relation to the situation (it is).

THE EXPERIENCE

1. EMOTIONS

How do people want to feel?

2. BENEFITS

What does the product have to provide to make people feel this way?

THE THING

3. FEATURES

How does the product deliver the benefits?

4. SENSORY CUES

What attributes do people associate with these features?

PREPARE COLLAGE EXERCISES

To get ready for the co-creation activity, we'll need to (1) create a canvas, and (2) produce a stimulus kit to give participants a way to express their ideas.

CREATING THE CANVAS

This is the blank slate that is used for people to place stimuli. Its main goal is to give people a way to think about what you are studying.

MY CURRENT EXPERIENCE INTERACTING WITH THE INFORMATION AND CONTROLS IN MY LUXURY VEHICLE AND HOW IT MAKES ME FEEL....

Please do not overlap words and images

WORDS & IMAGES HERE
↓

WORDS & IMAGES HERE
↓

POSITIVE EXPERIENCES

NEGATIVE EXPERIENCES

A canvas is typically a large piece of paper with the title and framework plotted on it. Ours are typically on paper 36" wide by 24" high. These dimensions are mere guidelines. The important criterion is that it can fit on a table and be easily reachable by the participant. If you don't have a plotter, you can write it on a piece of easel paper or poster board.

Sensory cue canvases need to have plenty of space for people to describe the chosen features using your stimuli. Since the canvas is made using a plotter, we tend to make it 42" tall. It is good to have 8"–10" of column width for each feature word.

Due to the pandemic, we have been conducting these activities using whiteboard tools such as Mural. There are many approaches to canvases. Feel free to find ones that work for you. Doing three words for a smaller project is acceptable and will be great for getting familiar with this activity.

Experience Canvas

My ideal **[insert product or service here]** experience is . . .

The barriers to my ideal experience are . . .

Features & Sensory Cues Canvas

My ideal **[insert product or service here]** is . . .

FEATURE	FEATURE	FEATURE	FEATURE	FEATURE	FEATURE
Full definition in this space, in case one word isn't enough.	Full definition in this space, in case one word isn't enough.	Full definition in this space, in case one word isn't enough.	Full definition in this space, in case one word isn't enough.	Full definition in this space, in case one word isn't enough.	Full definition in this space, in case one word isn't enough.

Every canvas has consistent elements:

TITLE

Experience canvas titles focus the participant on the situation. It can be the outcome of an existing situation or the desired outcome of that situation. Here are examples of experience canvas titles.

Sensory cue canvas titles tend to be straightforward. The most basic is: My ideal (product or service) is. . . . If you happen to know the benefits or desired outcomes the person is seeking, you might say, My ideal (product or service) that does (benefit) is. . . . If you have a specific use case or usage occasion in mind: My ideal (product or service) when I am (doing something) is. . . .

WORKSPACE

The simplest canvas structure is just a blank space. In this instance you are just asking people to describe a current or ideal experience.

A canvas can be structured to compare and contrast the experiences of today vs. the desired experience, current vs. ideal, the desired experience vs. the things that get in the way of the desired experience, ideal vs. barriers to the ideal. Another component of a structure to consider is time – some experiences comprise several discrete moments. Before, During, and After can be used to structure a current or desired journey.

A Sensory Cue canvas simply displays the features of the thing you want a person to describe. This is about how the thing you design will deliver the benefits people are seeking. Chapter 1 gives many examples of features. You can refer back to it to revisit the idea.

Here is a list of some features that might be brought to life: attractive, authentic, connected, convenient, customizable, delicious, durable, easy-to-use, effective, effortless, engaging, enjoyable, fresh, gentle, helpful, hydrating, innovative, luxurious, modern, motivating, multi-functional, personalized, powerful, practical, precise, premium, safe, smart, well-crafted.

Your workspace will simply have words like these. We have found it is best to keep the words you choose to bring to life to no more than six. Doing three words for a smaller project is acceptable and will be great for getting familiar with this activity.

CHOOSING FEATURES

At the highest level, sensory cues can be grouped into three feature categories: Useful, Usable, and Desirable.*

"Useful" pertains to the utilitarian or functional aspects of the thing. These are features like effective, smart, multi-functional, hydrating, powerful, practical, or connected.

"Usable" relates to how a person interacts with it. This would be features like easy to use, effortless, convenient, intuitive, or personalized.

"Desireable" is about the pleasant qualities the thing has that add delight to the experience. Delightful features are words like luxurious, engaging, enjoyable, attractive, or motivating.

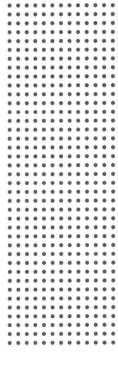

*Sanders, E.B.-N. (1992). "Converging Perspectives: Product Development Research for the 1990s." *Design Management Journal*, Fall.

In Homework 1, you (along with everyone else) told us that your **ideal sweet treat** is:

- Delicious
- Homemade
- Special
- Indulgent
- Premium
- Convenient
- Impressive

For this 2nd homework, we're taking those words and asking you to describe what each might look or be like if it were applied to **your ideal:**

- Hot Chocolate
- Baked Good
- Pudding

SELECTING THE RIGHT FEATURE WORDS

The words you choose to put on a sensory cue canvas need to be relevant to what you are seeking to design and be important to the situation. The words will describe how people want the benefits to be delivered. There are several ways to identify the words that make the most sense.

When making your selection it is best to have not just the words but what the words mean to people in relation to the area of focus and the situation. This helps you ensure that your feature choices don't have a lot of overlap. For example, easy to use, effortless, and convenient are closely related. Easy to use and luxurious are very different. You will have more design options when your words are differentiated.

A company might have brand pillars, which are the elements they want the brand to stand for in the minds of their target audience. These are usually feature words. Oftentimes companies have quantitative research that identifies key drivers of purchase. These drivers and pillars tend to be features. You can choose these. If you take this direction, you will want do an online activity to ask people what the words mean to them.

The most common approach we use is to ask people which words are most important for a given product or service. We typically do online activities where we give people a list of words and have them select the five or six most important words in relation to the situation. This can be done using any online survey tool. Once people choose the words, we have them define what the words they chose mean using the same survey.

Another approach we often use is feature mapping. After participants finish describing an ideal experience collage, we do the following quick exercise. People are given a blank canvas and pages of stickers with feature words. We have them choose the words that are important for the product or service to deliver the ideal experience. Participants take the words that are important and group them in a way that makes sense to them. These participant-made clusters allow you to see words that are related. Participants then explain each cluster and give it a name. These explanations can help you identify features to bring to life through a sensory cue activity.

Once you have identified the words, you want to select three to six words to bring to life. The more words you choose, the more interview time you will need to get explanations of the chosen stimuli.

Depending on the type of information that you want to gain from your research project, canvases can be broken down by:

My ideal **[insert product or service here]** experience is . . .

EMOTIONS & BENEFITS

An "I feel" or "I am" canvas used to describe an experience.

My ideal **[insert product or service here]** experience is . . .

The barriers to my ideal experience are . . .

COMPARE AND CONTRAST

Ideal and barriers to the ideal.

My ideal **[insert product or service here]** is . . .

FEATURE	FEATURE	FEATURE	FEATURE	FEATURE	FEATURE
Full definition in this space, in case one word isn't enough.	*Full definition in this space, in case one word isn't enough.*	*Full definition in this space, in case one word isn't enough.*	*Full definition in this space, in case one word isn't enough.*	*Full definition in this space, in case one word isn't enough.*	*Full definition in this space, in case one word isn't enough.*

FEATURES & SENSORY CUES

An "It is" canvas used to describe a product or service.

My ideal **[insert product or service here]** is . . .

BEFORE	DURING	AFTER

PROCESS

A canvas used to describe a sequence of events.

BUILDING THE STIMULUS KIT

Stimuli are the tools you give people to describe an experience or thing. These can be words, images, objects, sounds, smells, and screen animations.

Your stimuli are used to create the types of results we showed in chapter 1, Making Experiences Actionable. As we said, there are many different types of images that convey different ideas. Your choices for stimuli are based upon the information you are trying to generate.

Words

aluminum	canvas	carbon fiber
chrome	cobalt	copper
cork	diamond	gel
glass	gold	graphite
iron	latex	leather
nickel	nylon	platinum
polycarbonate	rubber	silicone
silver	steel	stone
teflon	titanium	tungsten
vinyl	wood	zinc

Physical Objects

Imagery

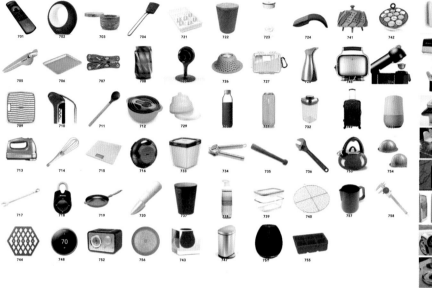

Digital Displays

Product Scents

Sounds

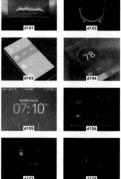

1 citrus 2 ginger ale

3 bubble bath 4 peach

5 clean clothes 6 lavender

7 rosemary 8 pecan pie

1 jingle bells 2 sonar vibration

3 two tone ding 4 bells

5 harp 6 weighted chimes

7 metal closing 8 liquid drop

SELECTING STIMULI FOR EMOTIONS

To describe an experience, a kit only requires words and images.

The goal is to identify the emotions associated with an experience and ground them in the specific context of the situation.

CONTEXTUAL WORDS

Positive and negative words can also be used to describe the context: clean, messy, crowded, empty, rainy, sunny, bright, dark. . . .

EMOTIONAL WORDS

The most common words used to describe experiences are emotional in nature. They are adjectives that express how the experience feels or should feel.

Situations that already exist (Current Experiences) tend to have both positive and negative elements. Therefore, a stimulus kit for this type of experience needs to have both positive and negative words.

Relaxed	Nervous
Independent	Afraid
In Control	Overwhelmed
Comforted	Ashamed
Focused	Confused

EXPERIENTIAL IMAGES

Experiential stimulus images tend to be abstract. They visualize the emotions or ideas related to an experience in an abstract and metaphorical way. Contextual images can be used to metaphorically describe what is happening. They do not have to be literally connected to what you are trying to understand. Selecting stimulus imagery follows the same principles as the words.

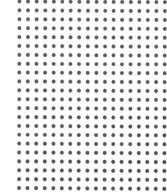

Positive emotional images   **Negative emotional images**

EXPERIENCE COLLAGING STIMULI

Try to keep the total number of images to less than 90; the same for the words. Ideally, you want as few words and images as possible, but you do not want to have so few that you leave out possible emotions and benefits.

A Current Experience set of words and images should include an equal number of positive and negative stimuli. This helps ensure you are not biasing participants' descriptions of the experience, positively or negatively.

Ideal Experience words and images are simply a subset of current experience stimuli. You only want positive words and images, as you are seeking to understand the desired outcome.

When using a compare and contrast combined canvas, your stimuli are once again a combination of positive and negative words and images.

MULTISENSORY STIMULI FOR FEATURES & SENSORY CUES

As the name implies, these kits engage all the senses that are relevant to the experience. The stimuli are used to describe how each feature should look, act, feel, taste, sound, and smell. Depending upon what you are making, you might not need to build a kit that addresses all five senses. These kits deconstruct the characteristics of a thing and give it to people as stimuli to reconstruct the thing in a way that is meaningful to them.

SENSORY CUE WORDS

These words help people describe the features that deliver the benefits in terms of how they look, act, feel, taste, sound, and smell. These are concrete, descriptive words. You want to come up with 5–6 sensory cue words that you think might describe each of your features.

"It Is . . ." Words

Big	Coated	Glossy
Boxy	Colorful	Lightweight
Bright	Contoured	Metallic
Clear	Curved	Polished

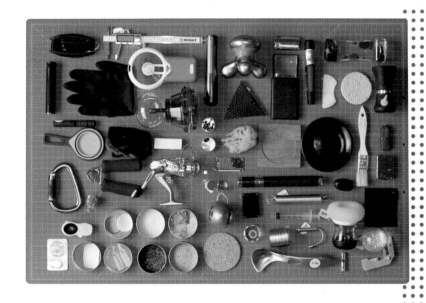

MULTISENSORY STIMULUI: OBJECTS

Objects can prove an effective addition to words and images. Using physical objects to engage the senses helps participants to step into feature-focused "It is . . ." conversations and think about how an ideal product or service should be.

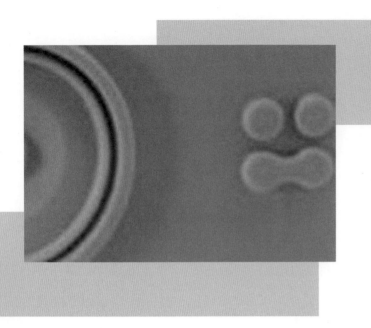

MULTISENSORY STIMULI: CHARACTERISTICS

What materials could the thing be made of? What color should it be? Should it be rough or smooth? Matte or shiny? Heavy or lightweight? Physical examples work best for this category.

MULTISENSORY STIMULI: ANIMATIONS

Dynamic visuals such as animations or video clips can articulate digital interfaces or components of an experience that cannot be articulated otherwise.

MULTISENSORY STIMULI: APPEARANCES

What does it look like? Is it hard or soft, masculine or feminine, traditional or modern? Give a wide range of choices. Use your design intuition.

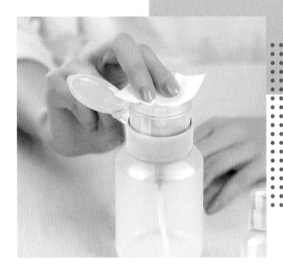

MULTISENSORY STIMULI: INTERACTIONS

Is it a digital or physical interaction? Is it a knob or dial or slide? Should it be sealed or tamper-proof? Think through all the possibilities of use. Find examples of multiple ways to deliver each interaction.

GETTING THE KIT STARTED

Here are some examples of categories you might use to start building a multisensory stimulus kit. The words shown are not the stimuli themselves, but rather prompts on what to look for. For example, to build a stimulus kit that will explore product packaging, you might think about the materials that the package could be made from, its shape and structure, or any graphics present.

STIMULUS CATEGORIES	PROMPTS	
PACKAGING	Materials the package is made of	Information on the package
PRESENTING INFORMATION	Diagrams	Instructions
WAYS TO CONTROL IT	Knobs	Buttons
WAYS IT TELLS YOU SOMETHING	Sound	Animation
THE SOUNDS SOMETHING MAKES	Chirps	Screeches
THE WAY SOMETHING SMELLS	Clean	Putrid
PRODUCT BEHAVIORS	Things that happen when a button is pressed	The way parts move
FOOD	Recipe appearance and origin	Ingredients

PROMPTS

Information moving across a screen	Screen behavior	
Form or structure of the package	Graphics on the package	Displays what is inside, if at all
Touchscreen	Voice control	
Lights	Physical feedback	
Beeps		
Refreshing		
Materials it is made from	Construction and how it is made	The sound parts make when they come together
Preparation	Serving and presentation	

SELECTING STIMULI

Building a stimulus kit requires a designer's intuition. It is one of the most subjective things you will encounter when preparing collage exercises. Building the kit requires you to imagine how you would like the product or service to be, almost as if you were designing it yourself.

In most cases, your stimuli should be outside the category. Selecting stimuli outside of the category enables participants to think past the current experience and dream up their ideal experience. For example, if you were co-creating the ideal printer, you would not want to use printers as stimuli for a collage activity. Instead, pull ideas from an adjacent category such as consumer electronics.

There are many ways to find stimuli. You can search online, go to a store and purchase items, or pull from an existing collection. Generally, our team has found that the best way to create a stimulus kit is to simply start picking. Every stimulus you select will inspire more ideas.

Personality

Look & Feel

Objects

Displays

Examples of stimulus groupings

GROUPING STIMULI

You want to organize your stimuli into logical chunks to present them to people. These chunks will be similar to the previous section where we showed you various ways to deconstruct something. For example, you might have a chunk of stimuli related to materials.

Presenting stimuli in the form of logical groupings helps participants step into the activity. For each group, you can let the person know how you want him or her to think about the stimulus.

Physical stimuli can be interpreted in a variety of ways by participants. We tend to group them all into one category.

EDITING STIMULUS GROUPS

Once you have gotten your kit together, you will need to edit it. We tend to have 10–15 stimuli per category or grouping. It is common to have too many stimuli and need to cut back. Try to avoid having multiple items that communicate the same thing. Since this is exploratory research to discover what is possible, you want to have a range of different ideas as opposed to similar ideas.

PRODUCING THE STIMULUS KIT

Once you have your stimulus kit assembled, you need to get it ready to present to participants.

It is preferable to do sensory cue interviews face to face so that people can touch things and interact with stimuli. Virtual interviews can be done as well, but you lose the sense of touch and smell, and the ability to interact with objects.

NUMBERING STIMULUS

You need to number all the images so that you can refer to them when people select something. This is also important for your analysis. We will cover those details later.

For physical stimuli, you might want to put numbers on stickers and then put the stickers on the objects. We typically photograph the stimuli and put the pictures on stickers for in-person interviews. When a person selects something, you can capture the data by placing the sticker in the appropriate location on the canvas.

For virtual interviews, you can import the numbered images into Mural and use them like stickers.

Numbered Stimuli

CONDUCT COLLAGE EXERCISES

It is important to present your activities to people in a way that enables them to easily step into the situation you want them to describe. For all of the approaches we have discussed, you want to start by introducing the canvas since it serves as the framework for what you are asking people to do.

EXPERIENCE COLLAGE BUILD

When presenting current, ideal, and combined canvases, you want to start by presenting the title. Once you have explained the title, you will want to describe the connection between the title and the canvas structure. Each section in the structure impacts the way the title will be perceived by the participant.

When presenting desired experience activities, it is extremely important to make sure participants understand you are not asking them about the world as it is today. Make sure you emphasize that it is about their experience in a perfect world.

Once a participant understands and connects with the canvas, you can present the stimuli. You want to let people know that they can use words or images in each area of the canvas. You need to tell them to only use the words or images that are relevant to them (not all the stimuli). To get started, encourage the participant to look through the stimuli. Let the participants know that if they see a word or image that looks like it relates to one of the canvas areas, place it there.

"IDEAL ME" ACTIVITY FOR SENSORY CUE EXERCISES

When research participants engage in an ideal experience activity, they become aware of the desired outcome. We refer to this as an aspirational mindset. People are free to see the category not as it exists today but as they would like it to be.

Getting participants in an aspirational mindset is key to enabling them to engage in a sensory cue activity in a way that enables them to make and describe their ideal product, service, process, or journey .

We often do an abbreviated version of desired experience collaging prior to this activity. It can be as simple as having people choose three images that describe how they want to feel in the situation.

You want them to imagine the end result of living with the product or service you design. The person needs to imagine how he or she ideally wants to feel when using it. The best way to do this is with an ideal experience collage. You have already learned about this and hopefully made one of these exercises. When used with a stimulus kit, you only need about 10 words and 10 images. You don't want to take up a lot of time in your interview on this activity. It should only take 5–10 minutes for the person to build it and 5–10 minutes for the person to explain.

My Ideal **Decluttering Solution** for my Living/Family Room is...				
EASY TO USE	VERSATILE	ATTRACTIVE	DURABLE	ORGANIZED
EASY TO USE	VERSATILE	ATTRACTIVE	DURABLE	ORGANIZED
My Ideal **Decluttering Solution** for my Living/Family Room is...				

SENSORY CUE COLLAGE BUILD

You want to explain what you want the person to make by introducing the title. You can ask your participant why the ideal (what you are studying) is important to helping them feel the way that is expressed in the Ideal Me activity.

Next, you will go through the canvas words. For each word you have two key questions:

What does (feature word) mean in relation to your ideal (whatever you are studying)?

Why is (feature word) important for your ideal (whatever you are studying)?

Once the person has imagined how he or she wants to feel and starts to think about what the features mean within the context of what you are designing, you are ready to start what we call "the build."

Start with your sensory cue words. Have the person look them over. Let the participant know that if one of the words helps to describe the features for his or her ideal, they should place the word in the appropriate box on the canvas.

This should only take the participant 3–4 minutes to do. If you have any other words, you can present these next.

The most important thing when presenting your stimuli to people is that you understand how you deconstructed the elements of what you are studying. If you understand it, you can present it in a simple conversational way. You are giving them your chunks of stimuli so that they can build their ideal product or service.

Here is an example of how to explain to the participant how to use it.

"Here is the information you might want."

"The images here show how that information might be presented."

If you have screen animations, you might say, "Here are some ways the information might act or move on the screen."

Using a page with different types of controls, you could say, "Here are some ways you could tell it what to do."

Again, the key point here is you are connected to your stimuli, have it chunked out in a logical way, and can explain it simply.

Tip: *Throughout the build, you always want to do a few things:*

- *Constantly reinforce the context of the study, whether it's for their ideal or current experience.*

- *Remind people to only pick the things that truly relate to their ideal.*

- *Encourage participants to only pick things that jump out at them right away.*

- *Participants will ask what the stimulus is. Don't tell them. Avoid creating bias and just say, "It's whatever it means to you."*

145

MODERATING AND NOTE-TAKING

Experiential and sensory cue moderation are quite different. They generate different types of data but can utilize similar note-taking templates.

MODERATION FOR EXPERIENCE EXERCISES

Once a person has made the collage, it needs to be explained by the participant. Your goal is to understand what the emotions mean within the context of what you are studying. For both current and ideal discussions, you are trying to understand the situation, and what is causing or needs to cause the emotional outcome. Make sure you ground your discussion in what it is you are designing.

For current experience discussions you might ask, "What is happening that causes you to feel that way?"

During ideal experience moderation you might ask, "How does that relate to your ideal _____ experience. What do you want to happen?"

NOTE-TAKING FOR EXPERIENCE EXERCISES

When note-taking for the collage discussion, you will want a template. Along with the typical note number, note, and participant number columns, you will want columns for stimulus and canvas location.

You do not need to write down everything the participant says. It might take a few probes to get to a clear understanding of the experience. Once you understand what is happening and the emotional impact, or what should happen and the desired emotional state, you can capture it. You might need to ask the participant to restate this once it emerges in the conversation. You want to make sure that you capture the ideas in their words.

When the person explains the collage, it is a good idea to list out the details of the experience. This will be important later.

SENSORY CUE MODERATION

After doing the Ideal Me activity and the build, you should have used about an hour of time. We typically schedule 3-hour interviews. You should have about two hours left to understand what the person made. We find that people often need a bathroom break, cup of coffee, or a snack around midway through the interview.

Once the build is completed, you want to have your participant explain every stimulus that was chosen. Sensory cues are concrete, so you need to get a very detailed explanation. You want to understand how the cue relates to the feature and what details of the stimulus embody the cue.

Imagine you need to fill in the words for this page in order to describe what all of these cues mean in relation to a feature. Your moderation of your participants is what is required to accomplish this. When I moderate these activities, I always imagine I am writing the words for the deliverable. I've made the mistake in the past of not getting these details and therefore had gaps in the deliverable.

Here is an example of how to moderate a sensory cue conversation:

CUSHIONED
My ideal tools have handles that are cushioned to protect my hands or absorb shock.

Soft Material
The material is soft and flexible with some give, like rubber or silicone.

M: Tell me about "cushioned." How is "cushioned" related to "ergonomic"?

P: It protects your hands to absorb shock.

M: Can you point to any of the stickers that say cushioned?

P: That one.

M: What about stimulus 321 (number code) says cushioned?

P: It has a material that is soft and flexible like rubber or silicone.

M: Can you point to the part of image 321 that is telling you it's cushioned?

P: The handle.

M: What about the handle says "soft and flexible"?

P: It has some give when you squeeze it.

P Participant ▓ Descriptor Questions

M Moderator ▓ Connector Questions

This conversation might seem strange – moderating this type of exercise requires us to ask extremely obvious questions. It's important to have participants explain their ideas in their words to avoid bias. Give participants time to think, and if they're having difficulty explaining, try rephrasing the question.

So really that's it. Just keep asking the same types of questions over and over for each stimulus. It's not difficult. It just requires thoroughness and dedication. You will find after a few stimulus explanations that people start to learn what you want them to explain. It gets easier for you, but they still have to give you lots of details.

It is also important to realize there are two types of conversations that can be had during this moderation.

Descriptor conversations: these discussions are when you ask a person to define or describe a sensory cue, feature, benefit, or emotion.

Connector conversations: in this case you are asking someone to explain a relationship or connection between a sensory cue and a feature, a feature and a benefit, or a benefit and an emotion. These conversations are very important for experience modeling. They help you make connections that can be expressed in your framework. We will cover this more in chapter 9, Finding the Big Ideas.

As we discussed in chapter 4, Having Effective Conversations, it is important to be thoughtful and intentional when you moderate by knowing the conversation you want to have. These conversations are key when moderating sensory cue exercises.

The final step in this moderation are connector questions between the feature words and the ideal experience. In this case you want to ask a question such as:

If you had your ideal [thing you are studying] with the qualities like you have imagined in [feature box 1 with stickers], how would that help you achieve your ideal experience?

Their answer. . . .

Why would it make you feel that way?

Their answer. . . .

You want to do this for each feature box on your canvas.

When doing this you can also ask your note-taker to help you by listing some of the ideas that came out of the sensory cues in that feature box i.e., cushioned (from our previous example).

NOTE-TAKING FOR SENSORY CUE EXERCISES

When note-taking for the sensory cue discussion, you will want a template that is similar to an experiential one. It will have the typical note number, note, and participant number columns along with columns for stimulus, and canvas location.

You do not need to write down everything the participant says. It might take a few probes to get to a clear understanding of what the stimulus means in relation to the feature. Once you understand what it means and what the specific details of the sensory cues are, you can capture all of it. You might need to ask the participant to restate this once it emerges in the conversation. Again, you want to make sure that you capture the ideas in their words.

1. EMOTIONS
How do people want to feel?

2. BENEFITS
What does the product have to provide to make people feel this way?

3. FEATURES
How does the product deliver the benefits?

4. SENSORY CUES
What attributes do people associate with these features?

EXPERIENCE COLLAGING AS HOMEWORK

Collaging exercises can also be conducted as homework. "Homework" refers to giving participants an activity to be completed on their own, prior to a moderated research session. The purpose of homework is to efficiently prime participants on the subject of the study and efficiently collect preliminary data.

INSTRUCTIONS

When experience collaging is conducted as homework, you will need to include instructions. These instructions need to step people into the experience, describe how to use the canvas, and introduce the stimuli. Think about how you would moderate this exercise in-person, and integrate those instructions into the homework. It is important to explain to participants that they can select as many or as few stimuli as they want, but they should only use the words or images that are relevant to them. A good way to get people started is by encouraging them to take the first step of looking through the stimulus images.

EXAMPLE HOMEWORK INSTRUCTIONS

Thank you for participating in this study! Please read these instructions before starting the activities.

Here's what you can expect:

1) Before your interview, we ask that you complete this set of homework exercises. These are crucial for the interview, so these homework exercises must be completed and you must send us high-quality photos of all completed pages prior to your interview.

PART 1: MY CURRENT EXPERIENCE

On the following pages, please answer the questions about your current experience. This activity should take about 10–15 minutes to complete.

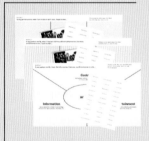

PART 2: MY IDEAL EXPERIENCE

After you complete Part 1, you will use stickers of images and words to describe aspects of your ideal experience. Part 2 should take about 15–20 minutes to complete.

2) During the interview, we will have a discussion about the homework exercises. Our conversation will be approximately 1.5 hours in total.

Email us for any questions!

CHAPTER 6 REVIEW

UNDERSTAND THE APPLICATIONS OF COLLAGING

Choose a collaging approach that aligns with your research objectives.

PREPARE COLLAGE EXERCISES

Each type of exercise requires a different canvas and stimuli customized to your research effort.

CONDUCT COLLAGE EXERCISES

The moderation questions have a different focus for each approach, but they can use a similar note template.

USING THE PRINCIPLES

RELEVANT

What you ask people to make needs to relate to the situation in which it will be used.

ASPIRATIONAL

Ideal Experience collaging is focused on understanding what people wish for. Sensory Cue collaging concentrates on defining the ideal thing.

HOLISTIC

These tools give you the ability to see the big picture of a current or desired experience and the details of the thing you are designing.

ACTIONABLE

Sensory cues are
concrete.

VISUAL

Images are used to
describe experiences
and things.

WHAT YOU CAN DO NEXT

Connect your experiential thinking to images. Begin to notice pictures that express the experiences of life; describe what is happening around a product, service, screen, or place; show things in context; communicate details about things.

CHAPTER 7:

Relevant Aspirational Holistic Rigorous Actionable Visual

UNDERSTANDING THE SITUATIONS OF USE

1 APPROACHES TO CONTEXTUAL INQUIRY

There are many ways to understand where your design will exist and what will happen around it. There are a few methods we use most often.

2 KNOW YOUR DOCUMENTATION OPTIONS

Plan on telling your story in your deliverable.

3 CONDUCT AN EFFICIENT & EFFECTIVE INQUIRY

Observations are an important source of data. Capturing data in context requires planning.

APPROACHES TO CONTEXTUAL INQUIRY

Context is the place, people, items, and information involved in using your design. It also includes what is happening, or the activities that will surround what you create. It is important to understand where your design will exist. By understanding the world where your design will be used, you can ensure that your solution integrates seamlessly into that world.

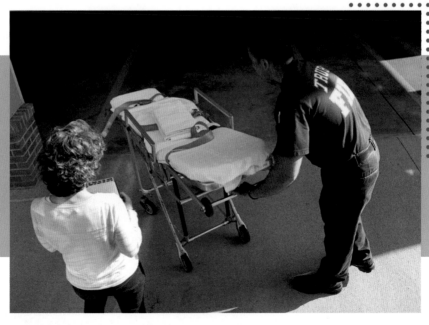

Contextual inquiry, often referred to as ethnography in the design world, can take on many different forms, and there are just as many differing opinions about what makes it successful. This type of research is about observing what is happening and asking questions along the way.

It's easy to spend a lot of time on contextual inquiry and arrive at very few actionable results. We will focus on the two approaches we use the most. We use these approaches because they are efficient and actionable.

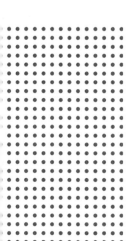

PROCEDURAL INQUIRY

Procedural inquiry is concerned with the steps involved in using what will be designed. We are trying to understand the entire process, so we want to capture all the actions a user takes to complete a given task. Digital interactions, medical procedures, installation steps, business processes, and setting up a product such as a new printer are a few examples where it might be important to understand what is happening in each step.

EXPERIENTIAL INQUIRY

Experiential inquiry is about understanding the definitive moments in a person's experience. In this approach, you want to understand the moments that stand out to the user while interacting with the product or service you are studying. It is similar to a procedurally focused approach, but in this case, we are letting the emotions drive the discussion instead of the process. We are learning about the experiences that happen around the subject of your study.

It is also important to understand aspirational desires – what the person wishes were happening and how the person wants to feel.

SELF-DOCUMENTATION

Both procedural and experiential inquiry can be accomplished by directing participants to do it on their own. Self-documentation is the method we use most often to understand context and use cases. Research participants are free to document things at relevant moments versus only doing things when you are present. This method results in less bias but sacrifices the ability to ask follow-up questions for deeper understanding.

Self-documentation is also very efficient. You can quickly gather more data with less effort than with in-person fielding. It's much more cost-effective than having a research team travel to fielding locations.

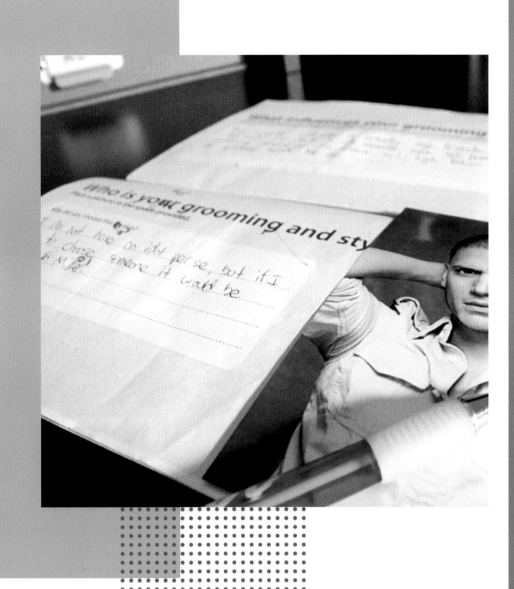

KNOW YOUR DOCUMENTATION OPTIONS

Planning for the deliverable is important. How you document the study influences the ways you deliver that information to the client later on. Finding the right way to document your inquiry has the power to bring context and current experiences to life.

Possible documentation methods include visual techniques, such as video or photography, and participant-led, self-documentation techniques.

VIDEO DOCUMENTATION

A video of your sessions gives you the opportunity to go back and review each process, or experience a walk-through at a later date. Inevitably, you will have questions about certain steps as you learn more. It's beneficial to have these recordings as a reference.

We find that clients like to see and hear firsthand how people use the products or services they provide, so keep this in mind when you have the option to document your contextual inquiry.

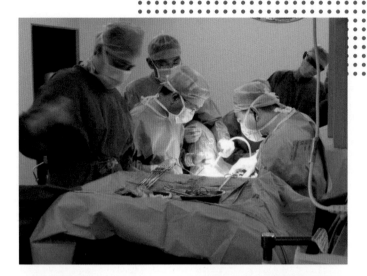

PHOTOGRAPHY

One of the simplest ways to capture context is to take pictures. You can use these as visual notes, and you will definitely want to include them in your deliverable. Photographs help bring many aspects of the context to life.

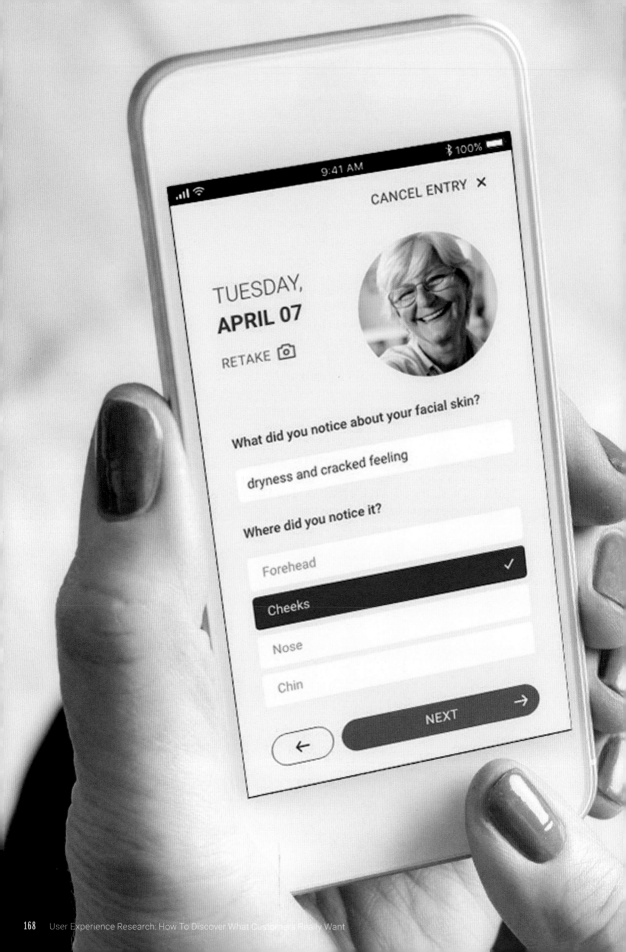

SELF-DOCUMENTATION APPS AND TOOLS

There are several apps available for self-documentation. We typically use dscout. The app allows people to document steps and moments with a picture or brief video. Each documented moment allows you to ask a set of questions.

You can also make a journal with questions about key moments. It would be similar to an app such as dscout. The biggest drawbacks are that people have to have the journal with them, if you use photographs they have to be mapped to the journal, and you have to enter all of the data into spreadsheet software to analyze it, whereas dscout already has the data entered and you simply have to export it.

One of the simplest ways to get context is survey software. You just ask people to list the places they use something, the people involved, the information that is used, the stuff they have with them, and so on. We often use this to get a quick understanding of a situation. The outputs are often used as a layer of stimulus in both experiential and sensory cue collaging.

CONDUCT AN EFFICIENT & EFFECTIVE INQUIRY

Along with asking questions, contextual inquiry involves observation. You want to watch what a person does, how their body interfaces with what you are studying, what items they are using, and how these items behave in relation to the tasks being performed. As you see the person doing activities and using things, you can probe for further clarification.

OBSERVATION GUIDE

A structured observation guide will serve as a checklist to ensure that you observe and discuss everything that might be important to the person. Keep it simple. A short list of questions is always best.

To Capture

- Context / Work Area / Environment
  - Tools
  - Artifacts
- Information used
- Who is involved / people in action
- Interactions between people, products, and systems
- Are there any workarounds?
  - Are they effective?
  - Are they efficient?

Probes for Observation

- Describe what you are doing in each of these steps.
  - Where are you doing it?
  - Are you using any tools?
  - Is anyone else involved? What are they doing? How often?
  - How long does this step take?
  - Do you enjoy anything about this step?
  - Is there anything you worry about?
  - What's most critical about this step?
- What are your main difficulties, and how do they affect your day?
  - How do you handle them?

Probes for Improvements/Solutions

- Are there similar products or systems that give you a more positive/negative experience?
- Are there any other products or systems that work well for you?
- Can you imagine how this could work better?
- What do you wish for?

GETTING GOOD DOCUMENTATION

THOUGHTFULLY FRAME YOUR SHOTS

If you plan to take videos or photos, you will need to consider how to frame your shots. You don't want to zoom in on the person or subject so closely that you lose the ability to capture the greater context. You also don't want to zoom out so far that you miss a detail. With practice, you will learn the best way to frame your story and find the balance between capturing enough context while still catching relevant details.

GET QUALITY CONTENT

If you're taking the time to create an engaging deliverable, you will need to have high-quality imagery supporting the story.

Videos and photographs need to be easy to see and well lit. Keep this in mind when documenting your sessions. Pay attention to the lighting. Do not shoot a video of a person in front of an exterior window. This will result in a silhouette. You don't want to make a video that looks like you talked to an undercover informant!

If you do record a video, you'll also want to have quality audio. Consider using lapel microphones or a tabletop microphone that can be placed near the discussion. Test the microphone before you use it.

> O
> O   **Tip:** *Learn how to use your cameras to get the results you need to tell the story. Take a photography class.*

TAKE NOTES

It is a good idea to have a designated note-taker. Analyzing session notes is much more efficient than going back and rewatching all of your video footage.

Have a note-taking strategy that works for the context you will be studying. Some locations are not good for laptop note-taking. You might be better off with paper and pencil.

If you don't have a note-taker, you might want to consider using an audio recording app and getting the file transcribed from an app. To get a good transcription, you will need good audio quality. Be sure to test your audio quality and transcription before you do your research. You never want to rely on something that might not work. Once your research is over, you will be stuck with the data you did, or did not, capture.

HAVE A SIMPLE SET OF KEY QUESTIONS AND DRILL DOWN

Procedural and experiential approaches require moderation. All of the principles we reviewed for moderation are used in both of these approaches. You will need to create a discussion guide. Your discussion guide should be a short list of questions that are consistently repeated for each step or moment.

Here are some typical procedural questions that can be applied to each step:

- What is happening?
- What is important for this step?
- What are your thoughts about this?
- What items are important?
- What information is required?
- What people do you interact with?
- Can you show me x?
- Can you point to x?

While understanding the procedure is the focus of this approach, it is good practice to add an experiential layer to the study by asking, "How does this step make you feel?"

To make your contextual inquiry even more actionable, you can add an aspirational layer by asking, "How do you wish you felt? What needs to change to make you feel this way?"

When studying moments, you want to quickly focus on what is meaningful to the participant and relevant to what you are studying. In this case you want to ask the person to think about the key moments that stand out in the experience.

Once you have a sense of the moments, you can go back and add detail with very similar questions, such as:

- How does this make you feel?
- What about the product or service is causing you to feel this way?
- What do you notice?
- What causes you to notice this?
- How do you wish you felt at this moment?
- What about the product or service needs to change to make you feel this way?

Your moderation needs to drill down into the specific details of the product or service that is causing the emotional outcome. Depending on your research goals, you might want to understand which step or moment is most important, most frequent, most time-consuming, most challenging, or the one people would most like to change.

Self-documentation requires a similar set of questions. It also requires very clear instructions to explain what you want people to do. The most important part of the instructions is making sure people have a clear understanding of what moments to document. It's a good idea to test these instructions out on a friend before you launch your study. If your instructions are not clear, you will be surprised with poor data in the end.

Here are some examples of self-documentation questions:

- What did you notice about [subject of study]?
- What caused you to notice?
- What did you do about it?
- How did it make you feel?
- What did you wish for?
- Who was there?
- What were the things involved?
- Where were you?

The right focus combined with the right questions can provide amazing clarity.

CHAPTER 7 REVIEW

APPROACHES TO CONTEXTUAL INQUIRY

Determine if it makes more sense to capture moments or processes. Decide upon the best way to get that information: do it yourself or have your participants do it for you.

KNOW YOUR DOCUMENTATION OPTIONS

Video and photography are important tools for capturing context. Self-documentation tools allow you to get this information without being there.

CONDUCT AN EFFICIENT & EFFECTIVE INQUIRY

Develop an observation guide. Be thoughtful about the imagery you capture. Think about how you will take notes in context.

USING THE PRINCIPLES

RELEVANT

Describes the situation of use.

RIGOROUS

Capturing data in context requires planning.

ASPIRATIONAL

Try to understand what people want to happen along with what is happening today.

ACTIONABLE

Identifies situations and
outcomes.

VISUAL

Telling a story about context
requires pictures and video.
Observation is a visual act.

WHAT YOU CAN DO NEXT

Observe people's behavior and interactions with things. What do you see? Imagine that everywhere you go you have to conduct research. How would you make that work?

CHAPTER 8:

 Relevant Aspirational Holistic Rigorous Actionable Visual

CONDUCTING RESEARCH

PREPARE FOR THE STUDY

Never underestimate how important it is to be ready when you show up in someone else's world.

FINALIZE YOUR SETUP

Make a list of everything you need to have ready and packed before you begin the field research. Be professional.

SOLIDIFY THE APPROACH

Test your research methodology to make sure it works.

PREPARE FOR THE STUDY

Before you begin conducting the research, or what we call fielding, you want to be sure you are completely ready.

Being prepared to get your data ensures you have no distractions, so that you can focus on actually conducting interviews. You are going to go meet someone you don't know and spend 2–3 hours with that person learning about his or her experiences.

You want to be able to concentrate without distractions. There can be many surprises when doing research. Eliminate the ones you can control. This is a very simple idea, but it really matters – it sets your project up for success.

FINALIZE YOUR SETUP

If you prepare everything for the study in advance, you free up thinking space so you can focus on getting the data. Here is a list of items to begin thinking about before your participant walks through the door.

PARTICIPANT IDENTIFICATION

Have a numbering system in place to identify each participant. This will be the participant number in your note-taking template. Before each interview, know the participant's number.

RECORDING

If you decide to record your interview, be ready to start recording as soon as you meet your participant. Make sure device batteries are charged.

For video recording, ensure all attachments and mounts are functioning. Practice quickly setting up your camera and framing the shot. Be sure to consider the environment for audio recordings. Will you be in a noisy location? If so, have a lapel microphone for yourself and your participant.

REMOTE FIELDING

Have a plan for using any technology like screen share or video conferencing.

Make sure your participant has an account and that they can log in before the interview starts. If your remote study will require participants to use digital whiteboard tools, think about how to familiarize them with the software and teach them how to use it. You don't want to waste valuable interview time with technical difficulties.

SUPPLIES

Make a checklist of all the supplies needed for the interview. Common items needed are: pens, high-lighters, notebook, note-taking template, discussion guide, extension cords, and recording equipment.

CONSENT FORMS

Participants must agree to do the research by signing their consent on a form. A consent form is a document that explicitly states a participant has agreed to the interview and any recordings. Here is an example of a basic consent form that can be adapted to fit your study.

Description

You're being asked to participate in a research study conducted by a design research team. We're conducting this study to better understand your preferences and experiences. The following information is provided to help you make an informed decision on whether or not to participate. If you have any questions, please feel free to contact the research team.

Requirements

The sessions are recorded for later analysis. Recordings are private and will only be used by the research team in order to inform changes based on your feedback.

In an effort to keep your personal information confidential, your identity will not be tied to your response in any publication or presentation of the results of this research.

Further, all ideas, suggestions, and proposals made by you in connection with your participation are voluntary. The research team is free to use all such ideas, suggestions, or proposals without obligation of any kind to you.

Your Rights

Your participation in this study is completely voluntary. You are free to refuse to take part or to discontinue taking part in this study at any time without fear of penalty.

Questions

If you have any questions about the study or any questions about your rights as a participant, you may contact the research team (see contact info below). If there is any part of this consent form that you do not understand, please ask the researcher before signing.

Researcher Name
000-000-000
researcher@email.com

Signature of Participant _____

Date of Signature _____

MODERATION

Familiarize yourself with the discussion guide and be ready to go off-script. Have an introduction prepared to ease your participant into the subject and review the moderation do's and don'ts from chapter 4.

EXERCISE MATERIALS

If you will be using a collage exercise as part of your interview, make sure everything is ready and accessible. Have a blank canvas accessible and stimulus packets printed and organized. Try to avoid fumbling around looking for things.

SOLIDIFY THE APPROACH

You want to have a repeatable process so that you can find patterns in the data. You don't want to make modifications to your methodology once you start fielding.

To prevent the need for modifications later, you should test your approach. This will help determine if people are relating to the subject as expected and if the method is generating the information you need to focus your design efforts. This testing process is called a "pilot."

Pilot testing allows you to modify your approach before you begin collecting data. This ensures your process will be repeatable. In almost all cases we find that we need to adjust our approach to ensure it is relevant and actionable.

To pilot your study, conduct your interview as if it were real. At the start of the interview, you might let your participant know that you're testing your approach, not the person. Once you get into the research activities, you might want to explore how the person is perceiving your questions or the canvas.

You might ask what the participant is thinking and let the person know what you are thinking or wanting to learn. Feel free to ask how they would say something in their words, such as the title on the canvas. These questions will provide insight into how to modify your approach.

After your pilot test, decide what modifications to make in order to refine your approach. If necessary, conduct another pilot to ensure the modifications have addressed your concerns. It might take a couple of tries to get it right, but that is okay. After piloting, you should have a solid plan that you can repeat over and over.

CHAPTER 8 REVIEW

PREPARE FOR THE STUDY

Eliminate the distractions you can control.

FINALIZE YOUR SETUP

There are many things to think about in an interview: consent, technology, data capture, and materials. Moderation is your main focus at this time.

SOLIDIFY THE APPROACH

Every research methodology needs to be refined before data is collected. In order to have a repeatable process, you can't modify your approach as you go.

USING THE PRINCIPLES

RELEVANT

Pilot testing ensures the research objectives will be addressed.

RIGOROUS

Refining your plan before you collect data allows you to have a repeatable process so you can identify patterns.

WHAT YOU CAN DO NEXT

Make a list of everything you will need. Practice setting everything up and taking everything down.

CHAPTER 9:

Relevant   Aspirational   **Holistic**   **Rigorous**   Actionable   **Visual**

FINDING THE BIG IDEAS

CODE THE DATA

Group together similar ideas from different participants.

IDENTIFY THEMES

Summarize similar ideas from different participants.

SYNTHESIZE THEMES

Group summarized ideas into buckets.

CODE THE DATA

Since you have developed an approach and repeated that approach across multiple participants, you are now able to identify common ideas across multiple participants. We have a structured process for doing this. The goal is to come up with a set of statements that fully capture the ideas that multiple participants have in common.

THE PATH FROM DATA TO INSIGHTS

Now that your research is completed, you need to find out what you have learned.

The quality of your final deliverable will be determined by how you analyze and synthesize your data. Analysis is where we break down notes to make sense of all the data gathered during fielding.

This broken-down data forms the building blocks of our final insights. The final insights provide our foundation for synthesis, where we organize those building blocks to craft a logical and coherent information structure that represents the data.

I. CLEANING DATA

Notes from all of your completed interviews.

II. CODING

Code your notes by similar ideas so you can focus on one theme at a time.

III. SORTING DATA FOR THEMING

Pull all the notes in each code together so you can focus on one code at a time.

IV. THEME SHEETING

Highlight ideas related to a code to find patterns. Summarize patterns with a theme statement.

V. BUCKETING

Group theme statements that share a common idea.

NOTE ID NUMBER

PARTICIPANT ID

TOPIC OR QUESTION

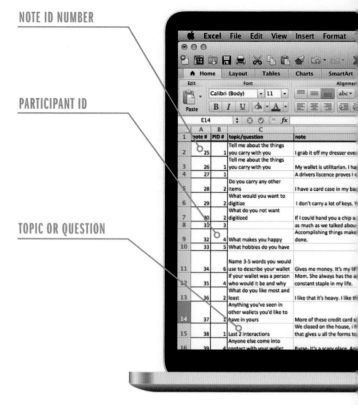

I. CLEANING DATA

Once you have completed all your interviews, you need to prepare your notes for analysis. We like to "clean" our notes by running spell-check. Then, we make sure other relevant information like data source, PID, and note number are filled in for every note.

Recall from chapter 5 that there are various columns in the note template. We will create a column titled "Code" that we will use to start breaking down our dataset. You will be working in and eventually filtering by this code column.

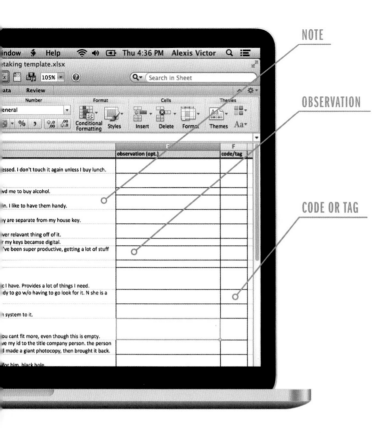

NOTE

OBSERVATION

CODE OR TAG

SORTING DATA FOR CODING

We typically have 1200 to 3000 lines of data on projects. Since we often use a combination of exercises and activities, we have different types of data that come from multiple sources. We might have context or current experience data from self-documentation, ideal experience data from a collaging activity, and "It is" data from a sensory cue exercise. Each of these different data sources is tagged in the section column of the notes.

Hopefully you have had an opportunity to familiarize yourself with Excel or Google Sheets. Your data is most likely organized based on the order of your interviews. The data from the first person you talked to is in the top rows,

and the data from your final interview is in the bottom rows.

You want to reorganize all your data and group it by section instead of by participant. Before you do this, make sure you have cleaned your data and added note and participant numbers. This is very important. Without these numbers you can't return your data to its original structure.

You want to select all your data and choose data>sort. This gives you the option to select the column by which you want to sort your data. Select the column letter for each section and sort your data.

Now you have similar types of data grouped together.

II. CODING (AFFINITIZING)

This is about grouping similar ideas to find common stories. Coding is a process that takes a large, disparate dataset and breaks it down into manageable chunks of like ideas to be further processed by "theme sheeting" (more on that later in this chapter). These chunks, or codes, contain similar ideas so you can focus on one theme at once.

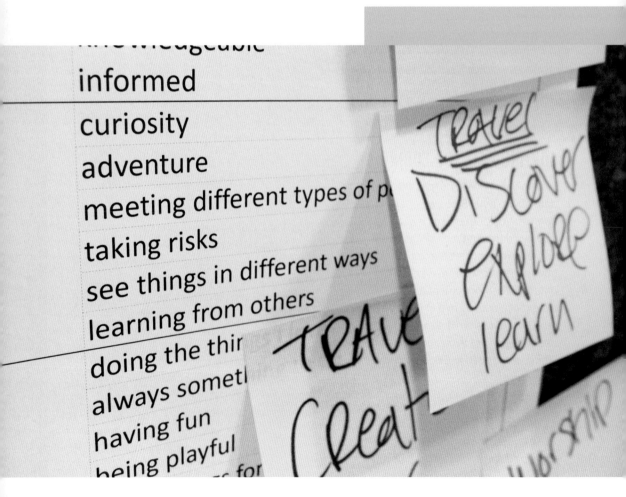

For example, one person might have said, "I want something that I can take with me everywhere I go." Another person might have said, "I want something that fits in my pocket so that it is easy to carry anywhere." Someone else might have said, "I want it to be easy to carry with me." Each has a similar story. In this case it's a story about portability or being easy to take with you.

Having been involved in the research, you probably have some idea of what these codes could be. Think about the things you believe you might have heard over and over.

To begin coding, read through all your notes in a given section. Pay attention to the stories and ideas in each section. As you read through these, you should start to notice similar ideas from different people. This will give you an idea of recurring themes or ideas that participants expressed. Begin writing down these themes; this will become your code list.

You will want to give each of these notes a similar code in the code column.

We find that in most of our studies, we end up with 20–30 codes. This of course depends on how big your dataset is, but conventional wisdom suggests keeping your code list descriptive, but not too descriptive. To code quickly, it helps to be able to keep the codes in your head or have them written on a single sheet of paper, and in our experience, 30 codes or less is the sweet spot.

A	
#	Code
101	Easy to use
102	Details
103	Customization/setting preferences
104	Gives me options
105	I like the design

Data Source:	Code #	Code Name:	Description of Code:
	A	B	C	D
Current Emoitions	201	Fear, Anxiety & Pain; Worry	I feel scared and nervous
Current Emoitions	202	No Control // Want to be in-control	I feel like I am not in-control
Current Emoitions	203	Anger & Dissapointment	I am angery and dissapointed in myse

CODE LIST

While reading through your data, you will want to make a list of the ideas you are seeing. These will be your codes. Once you've read through your notes and have a good idea of the recurring ideas, you're ready to build your code list.

Each code should have a name, definition, and number. Give the codes a descriptive name or phrase that will be memorable while you code.

Once you have built out your code list, you will want to number your codes. We typically use 3-number codes. The first number tags the type of data or where it came from in the interview. The last two tag the code in the code list. Going back to our previous example, you would have codes in the 100's for current experience, 200's for ideal experience, and 300's for "It is."

CODEBOOK

If you are dealing with a large dataset, or have a lot of people on your research team working on analysis, it is often helpful to develop a "codebook." A codebook expands on your code list to include other helpful information that ensures all coders are coding in the exact same way.

A few ways to do this include adding a definition to each code. For example, the definition of "portability" could be: anything you can take with you, is small enough to fit in a pocket, fits easily in the hand, and can slip into a purse/ bag/etc. If you have a lot of nuanced or similar data, including information on what should be included or excluded from the code is helpful. For example, small handheld items should be included in Portability, but items with distinct handles or grab points should be excluded because handles have their own code.

Tips: *Notes can have multiple codes. Just make sure to separate them by a comma.*

Include a description of the code to help all team members code in the exact same way.

E
What is in this code:
Being scared, having a scary physical feeling (like being suffocated), inflammatory/frightening words, being worried, anxious or nervous.
Feeling like you have no control over what is happening to you, feeling frustrated, lack of predictability, feeling burdened or restricted, can't quit bad habits, burdened, temptation, can't do the things I used to be able to do
Being mad or dissappointed in myself, anger at this situation in general, annoyance, shame.

F		G
Note		Code
A phone! iPhone, the 7 plus. I have a phone, but I want a bigger one. I don't know why bigger matters.		100
I usually spend it all on nothing I really need, I will buy toys. I get from doing chores and from my birthdays.		100
I have not to just spend and spend, don't want to spend it all. Also I learned that money is valuable.		100, 201

APPLYING CODES

Now that you have your code list with numbered codes and descriptive titles, or your detailed codebook, it is time to actually code your data. Start by creating a "Code" column in your spreadsheet. Then, read through each note and decide which code it best represents. Continue doing this until every last note is coded.

Now you simply go through your data and code each line. Most likely you will need to add codes as you go. Whenever you don't have a code for a new story or idea that emerges, you can add a code.

It is common to have data that needs multiple codes. Sometimes a note can represent two, three, or more codes.

When you have a piece of data that has two or more stories in it, just copy and paste that row of data. You can then add the additional code(s) as needed. Type the appropriate code numbers in your code column.

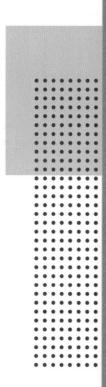

III. SORTING DATA FOR THEMING

Now you can use the "filter" function to only look at the data from a single code.

After you have coded all your data, you will count how many people mention each idea that you have coded. This allows you to only move forward with the ideas that 25–30% of the people had in common. So, if you talked to 10 people and three of them mentioned the idea of portability, you would move forward with that idea. If only one person mentions it, you would leave that idea behind.

Once all of your data is coded, you need to identify which codes patterned. We define a pattern as an idea that occurred from multiple participants. We use the cutoff of 25% to 30% of the participants. So, any ideas that emerged from 25–30% or more of the participants will be explored for themes.

You might see codes that have a lot of lines of data, but those lines of data all came from one person. These instances do not constitute patterns.

To find patterns you need to learn a few spreadsheet software skills. You want to learn how to do the "count" function in formulas. This will enable you to determine how many participants had data in each of your codes.

The other spreadsheet function you need to learn about is pivot tables. This feature allows you to select one of your codes and see how many times it was selected.

This saves you from wasting time on small theme packets. If you have not learned spreadsheet software yet, you can go through your smaller theme packets manually. If there are only one or two participants in each packet, you can get rid of them.

IDENTIFY THEMES

Once you have identified your codes that patterned, you will revisit those codes to further analyze the data. The goal is to identify specific insights that exist across multiple participants. These will be written into "theme statements" that accurately capture each idea.

Having themes based upon multiple participants helps ensure your credibility. It's important that people believe your conclusions.

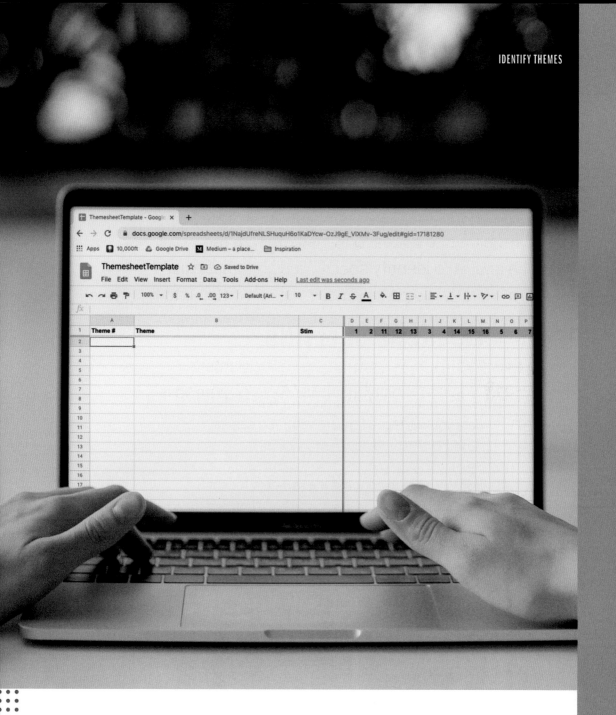

This is a theme sheet. It can be digital and done in spreadsheet software or created with pen and paper. Choose whatever you prefer. Theme sheeting requires dedication and focus for several hours at a time, so choose the format that will keep you the most focused and minimize distractions. It's best to get comfortable and not get up for a while when you do this. Once you get focused, it's best to finish a packet. It's also a good idea to have a highlighter.

IV. THEME SHEETING

You will need the raw data column and the participant number column. This is all of the data you will move forward with. You can say "Good-bye" to your low-frequency data.

You will need to print out the raw data for each high-frequency code. Using the code column you created, go down your list of codes and filter for each one in turn. For example, say your "Portability" code is number 302. Filter your code column for any instance of 302 (even if other codes are noted as well). You should be looking at only the notes from code 302. Now, print out all those notes in what we call a "theme packet." You can also export a PDF for each of your codes or just continue using the spreadsheet software if you prefer to work completely digital.

You are going to identify single ideas or themes that patterned across multiple participants. This will serve as the foundation for your deliverable.

Read through your theme packet, keeping your code definition in mind. Since you most likely had some data that received multiple codes, you want to look at your theme packet data through the lens of your code that patterned. Highlight the ideas that relate to that code.

While you are highlighting, you will begin to notice patterns of ideas, or themes, that keep occurring. Write these on your theme sheet, one idea per row. Once you have highlighted all the data in your packet, you will use your theme sheet to identify the different ideas and tag the participants these ideas came from. You want to count up the ideas that are in each of your theme packets. You do this by writing the participant numbers in the rows of your theme sheet next to the idea that is emerging. When you come across a new idea, you can add it to your theme sheet. It is important to not just make the theme statements, but to track who is saying what, so that you can move forward with only the "high-patterning" or "high-frequency" data, versus using one-offs and every little insight.

When you are finished with your packet, count the number of participants associated with each idea to identify the high-patterning ideas, that is, ones that came up in 25–30% or more of your participants. The ideas that have enough people behind them will be developed into theme statements. You can look through the ideas that did not have enough people and see if any can be combined to create additional themes.

Tip: It's best to get comfortable and not get up for a while when you do this. Once you're focused, try to finish a packet. It's also a good idea to have a highlighter.

THEME NUMBER

Record a number for each pattern so you can refer to them if you reorganize.

CODE

Record ideas or themes that keep occurring while reading through your theme packet.

STIMULUS NUMBERS

If you used stimulus, record the image number to refer to when bucketing themes.

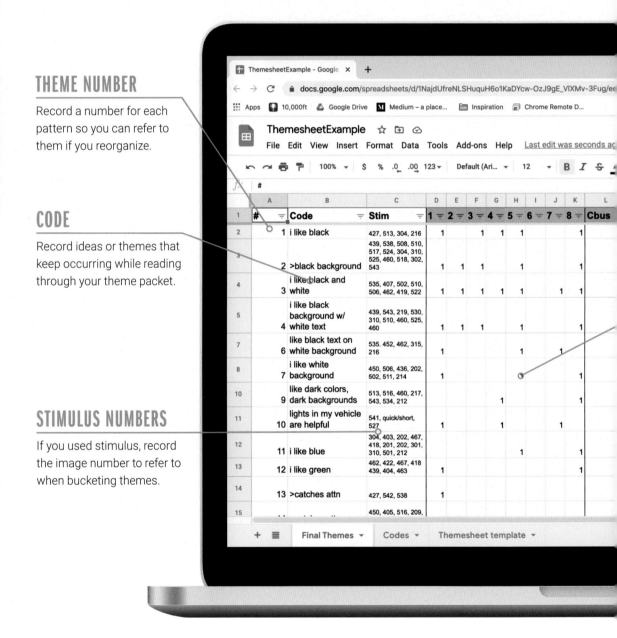

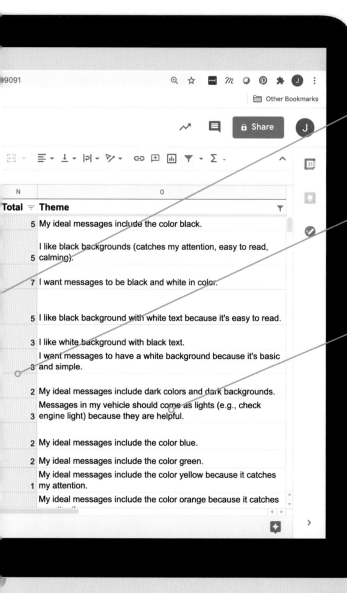

PARTICIPANT COUNTS

Put a 1 if your participant aligned with the theme.

TOTALS

Use the sum function to track how many participants aligned with the theme.

THEME STATEMENT

Create a complete sentence out of each pattern (see next page for rules and examples).

409	602	No Robots	
409	603	No Robots	the food is made fromscratch from start to finish, made with care is mad...
558	401	Hands On Prep	I like the handwriting on the package, the level of detailed in describing (smoked garlic rather than just garlic) - the handwriting makes it seem h
558	403	Hands On Prep	handwritten is timeconsuming so clearlysomeonecares about thatprodu
622	503	Hands On Prep	hand written labels communicate an extra level of care to me, it indicate caretome
558	201	Hands On Prep	it looks like a small batch thing, its not cheap, the handwritten ingredier communicate small-batch and not mass produced - things that aremade involve more time and hands on craftsmen focus, vs massmanufacturing and made without care
		Hands On Prep	the imagery focuses on ... and doing things

THEME STATEMENT EXAMPLES

EMOTION	SOLUTION
I want to feel independent as I grow older, like I can take care of myself without burdening my family.	I want the landing page to point me in the right direction and guide me so I can easily complete tasks on my own.
I want to feel motivated to save and build up a financial cushion because I know that the future can be uncertain.	I want my apartment building to have a small grocery or convenience store so I can quickly grab food as I leave or enter my home.

scratch

edients
le

The packaging communicates Made with Care to me when I see handwritten ingredients and details.

batch and

e box
atch
er quality

The packaging communicates

THEME STATEMENTS

Each of your themes that patterned will be converted into complete statements. Each statement needs to have a single message, be clear, and be actionable or inspirational. A well-written statement captures both "what it is" and "why it matters." We write theme statements in the first person to represent the voice of the user. It is very important that you stay true to the data when writing statements. Don't make things up.

Keep your final theme statements with your theme sheets in case you need to refer back to them and see how data laddered up to the theme.

CURRENT	PROCESS
I feel frustrated with my medical progress because I am trying to get better (eating well, taking my medications), but I am still not seeing results.	Before I was diagnosed, I noticed symptoms and went to my doctor.
Currently, I learn about savings opportunities by talking to an advisor or visiting my local branch because I trust people more than websites.	During the "purchase" step, I want to know how much money I have saved with my coupons or points before I swipe my credit card.

THEME PAGES

Once you are done making theme statements, you need
to get them into a format that can support "bucketing."
We will call these "theme pages." Bucketing is what we
call the process of affinitizing theme statements into
larger "buckets" or groups of similar ideas (more on this
in the next section). The buckets will eventually become
the foundation of your experience model.

Theme pages need to have information on them that
allows you to easily refer back to the raw packet data
where the statement originated. In many cases you
need to go back to the original notes and ensure you
understand the statement correctly.

Tip: *It is a good idea to color-code each page based
upon the type of data it represents: current experience,
ideal experience, context, etc.*

EXAMPLE THEME STICKER

Color code/Category
Theme Statement typed in a complete sentence.
Codes, tags, supporting information   Stimulus

We have software that automates the creation of these pages. These can be printed onto sticker paper or exported into Mural, a digital-first visual collaboration platform. You will need to find a quick way to create these pages so you can see all of your data and begin organizing it.

Some ways we have done this include:

- Typing them out and then printing and taping/pinning them up.
- Writing out your theme statements on large Post-it® notes.
- Creating them in a digital workspace.

Once you have made these pages, you need to put all of them on a whiteboard or get them into something like Mural or Miro.

When printing themes on half-page stickers, we tear the top third of the sticker backing off in order to make something that can stick on a whiteboard.

AWAY FROM HOME EXPERIENCE — THEME NUMBER: 169 — PARTICIPANTS: TOTAL: 4, SS: 1, PP: 3 — CONVENIENT

A product is convenient if it has carrying loops, straps, hooks, or clips so I don't forget it at home

ASSOCIATED STIMULI:
221   238   323   228

SYNTHESIZE THEMES

The goal of synthesis is to organize and group theme statements in a logical way that tells a coherent story. When we say "tell a story," we mean truthfully represent the data in a way that can be easily understood.

We typically have 150–300 theme pages for a project. These patterned findings are the pieces of the story. The story should be simple enough to put on a one-page framework when we begin Insight Translation. Think of it as your elevator pitch.

V. BUCKETING

To begin organizing the story, we create "buckets." A bucket is a group of theme statements that share a common idea. The purpose of creating buckets is to consolidate ideas and express relationships in the data. Your one-page framework will be based on your buckets. Each bucket will serve as a chapter of your story.

Start by grouping themes that have similar ideas. When you read each theme, decide if it fits into an existing bucket or if it is the start of a new bucket. If you are not sure where it goes, start a new bucket. Just like theme sheeting, don't force a theme into a bucket if it doesn't fit.

Going back to the anatomy of an ideal experience, recall that there are "It is . . ." elements, "I feel . . ." elements, and "I am . . ." elements. Group themes into these types of buckets. These categories will be useful when building your story.

Once you have a draft of your buckets, go back and review each bucket theme by theme to make sure they all work together. If you have any outlying theme statements, now is when they need to find a home.

Bucketing is an extremely iterative process. Don't spend too much time on the first pass; focus on roughing out the buckets.

COMBINING BUCKETS

As your buckets begin to take shape, you need to focus on the number that you have. Ideally, shoot for around 6–10 buckets. If you have too many buckets, look at combining some. We often take several buckets and combine them into a single bucket that captures their relationship. If you have a bucket with one or two themes, you can move those themes into another bucket. It's also entirely acceptable to have buckets within buckets to retain important distinctions.

NAMING BUCKETS

You can give your buckets working titles at any time. Don't spend a lot of time on the titles until you are done because the bucket might change or even be eliminated.

Once you feel your buckets are working and you have a story to tell, you can name them. Since you made different buckets for "I feel" themes vs. "It is" themes, you need to apply that thinking to your buckets. Your "I feel / I am" buckets need to complete that phrase. Your "It is" buckets need to complete that phrase as well. When you have your titles done, you should be able to read them and easily get a sense of your story.

You are now ready to build your one-page framework. We will discuss this further in the next chapter.

DO	DON'T
Be data-driven. If you need to go back to the data and check things, you can. We do that a lot. In many cases your themes might need to be refined. It takes practice.	**Inject bias**. Stay true to the words of the participants. If you have a theme that seems like it goes in multiple places, it might need to be broken up into single ideas or rewritten.
Bucket by data types. Organize themes that complete similar statements (e.g., "It is . . ."; "I want to feel . . .")	**Jump to solutions.** Once you define what people want, you can figure out what to do.
Eliminate a bucket if it is not working. Move themes that don't seem to fit into a parking lot. You can revisit them at the end and find a spot for them.	**Bucket based on what you would do as a designer.** This is not a to-do list. It's a story.
	Get emotionally attached to your buckets. Focus on the story you are making. Does it make sense?
	Bucket alone. Successful synthesis is a team effort.
	Get hung up on one theme statement. If you don't find a place for it, put it in the parking lot.
	Try to win an agreement. This is not a critique. Don't defend buckets if they leak. Fix them until everyone agrees.
	Confuse frequency of themes with importance of themes. Frequency of themes does not make them more important. Unless you've added this method into your approach, there is no data to show the importance of one theme or bucket in relation to another.

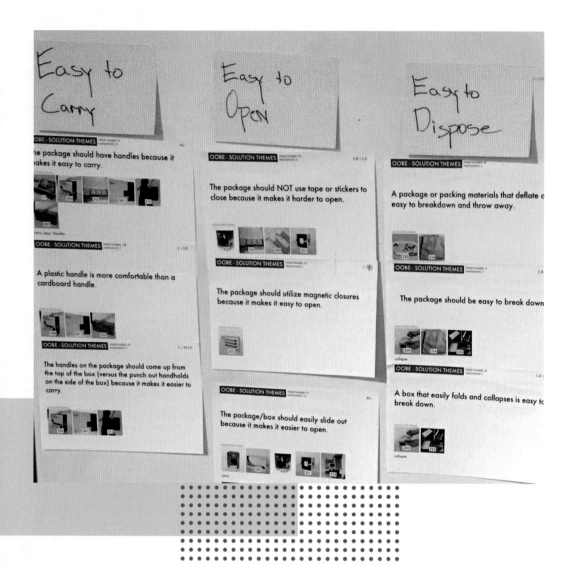

This is a really great time to learn. You chose and built your methodology. You executed your methodology using a repeatable process. You analyzed your themes. You have immersed yourself in the themes you made. This is the story you are stuck with. Inevitably there will be bits and pieces in your story that you wish you had. Think about what is missing and how you would go about creating that information. Remember this the next time you build an approach.

CHAPTER 9 REVIEW

CODE THE DATA

Codes describe the various stories that live in the data. Creating and using codes enables you to group similar ideas together.

IDENTIFY THEMES

Themes are singular insights formed from 25% or more of your participants. These are the building blocks of your story.

SYNTHESIZE THEMES

Bucketing organizes your themes into chapters. Reducing the components in your story enables you to build a one-page framework.

USING THE PRINCIPLES

HOLISTIC

Coding groups data into emotions, benefits, features, and sensory cues.

RIGOROUS

Identifying patterns in your data that occur across multiple participants ensures your findings are representative of the real world.

VISUAL

When analyzing data from projective techniques, you are identifying what the stimuli mean. Putting stimulus data on theme sheets helps organize the story based upon common visual themes.

WHAT YOU CAN DO NEXT

Keep learning spreadsheet software. Make sure you can do everything in this chapter using the software of your choice.

CHAPTER 10

Relevant   Aspirational   Holistic   Rigorous   Actionable   Visual

TELLING THE STORY OF THE FUTURE

MODEL EXPERIENCES

Organize research findings into a one-page framework.

DESIGN SOURCEBOOKS

Structure a deliverable that explains what you have learned in your research.

CREATE STORYBOARDS

Bring the story of the future to life.

MODEL EXPERIENCES

The primary purpose of a model is to communicate the user's story in a clear and digestible way. You've already collected insights about your user's experience, so now it's time to organize that information to make it shine. Modeling data to create a framework makes it easier to visually communicate an experience by simplifying the presentation of complex information.

A framework also ensures that your story is concise, making it more likely to be read and used. It allows you to put all the big ideas identified in your analysis and synthesis on a single page. It is the elevator pitch that represents hundreds of insights. We all know information overload can be paralyzing, so help your reader understand your findings by summarizing the story on a single page.

And, finally, diagrams are an efficient way to tell complex stories by articulating relationships. Your research project will deliver insights that have a definable relationship, like causality, hierarchy, or sequence. Diagrams allow you to describe how multiple themes relate to one another. For example, accurate information might ladder up to a feeling of safety.

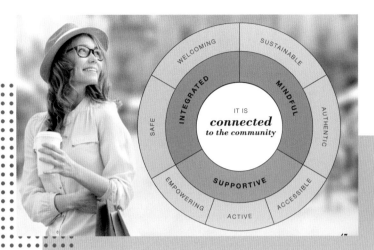

Describe how a new development should integrate into its community.

Describe the life-level aspirations that motivate millennial consumers.

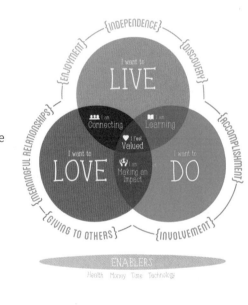

Describe the ideal benefits and features of ideal car controls and displays.

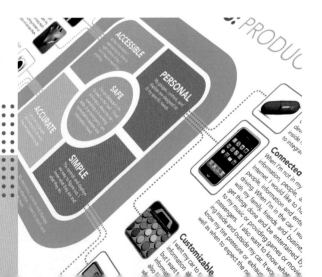

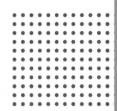

ANATOMY OF AN IDEAL EXPERIENCE

Before getting started with modeling, let's review the fundamentals of the Anatomy of Experience. Our framework links design attributes to user emotions through features and benefits. The connections between them ensure that research insights can lead to innovative products and services.

1. EMOTIONS

At the core of an experience, there are the Emotions. Any interaction with a product, service, or system results in an emotion. We believe that these emotions are the things people remember about interacting with your brand, making them the key to long-term engagements. We subscribe to the philosophy that "It's not about what you make, it's about how you make people feel." Emotional insights are "I feel" statements.

2. BENEFITS

The Benefits are then the direct tie between the product, service, or system and the emotion. They can be "I am" statements. For example, "I feel safe because I am focused on the road." The key benefit is "focused." They also can be "It is" statements. For example, "I feel confident because my phone will never break." The key benefit is "it will never break."

3. FEATURES

Now, people have specific ideas about how they want the key benefits to be delivered. These would be the Features of a product or service, which are typically specific functions, technologies, or interactions, such as touchscreen, gestural interface, or shock-proofing.

4. SENSORY CUES

Finally, there are specific attributes or Sensory Cues (such as, how it looks, feels, smells, tastes, or acts) that signal that the product, service, or system has the features that the users desire.

THE PROCESS OF MODELING

Modeling is an iterative process. It takes several rounds to find the perfect visual representation of your data, let alone make it fit on a single page.

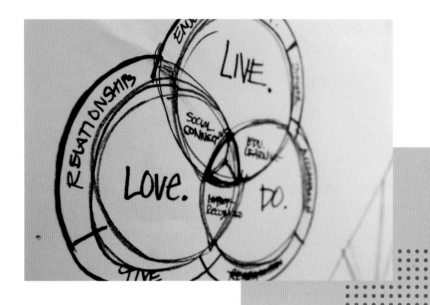

1. SKETCH

Have your team explore and sketch out the relationships in the data by testing different modeling approaches. Look for the connections between your synthesized buckets and let the data speak for itself.

2. ITERATE

Have your team share and compare their sketches. Based on how everyone visualized the insights, your models could end up looking very different. What elements do the sketches have in common? Are there any new ideas or connections? Align on a direction for your model and ensure that it's accurately interpreting what participants said during the study.

3. RENDER

Once you've arrived at a final model that accurately represents the data, bring the sketch into your preferred design program and polish it for your deliverable.

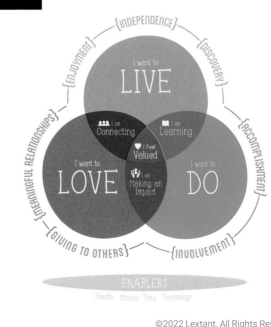

TYPES OF MODELS

Always let the data lead your design. If the research revealed a linear process, a layered model might be best. If the data is about the anatomy of an experience, a radial model might be a more appropriate visual. Here are a few examples of model designs:

LAYERED MODEL

These models use structures that show elements that stack or build on each other. They can depict both hierarchy and sequence. Layered models are useful for modeling user journeys.

CLUSTERED MODEL

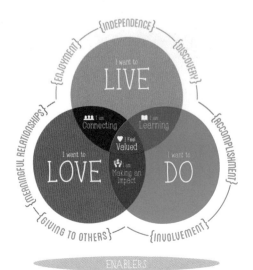

These models use clusters that overlap and indicate shared sets, interest, or responsibility. Sometimes they form a new shape or area within the overlap.

RADIAL MODEL

In these models the outer elements connect with a central element to hold the family together. Radial models can be used in combination to describe steps in a sequence of an ideal experience.

Total Beauty Experience

My Complete Routine
Taking care of myself is enjoyable. I clean everywhere deeply, kill and prevent the spread of germs, hydrate my skin, protect my skin, hair, and teeth from damage, and enhance how I look.

IT IS EXCITING
It's soothing and invigorating. It's easy to create new looks. Every detail is an expression of me.

IT IS EFFECTIVE
It's safe and proven to work, using the latest technology that's powerful, long lasting, and right for me and my needs.

IT IS EFFORTLESS
My routine is quick and easy to get the results I want, wherever I want.

I AM REJUVENATED
My mind, body, and spirit are relaxed and energized.

I HAVE THE LOOK I WANT
My look fits me and reflects my personality. It's right for the moment.

I FEEL ATTRACTIVE
I feel confident around others. I'm noticeable, desireable, and make a good impression on others.

I FEEL CONFIDENT
I know I look put together and can accomplish anything. I feel good and can appreciate life.

DESIGN SOURCEBOOKS

Why take all the time to share your research in a book format? At a fundamental level, it's because a book adds value. But really the answer is threefold:

TELLS A STORY

First, a book takes the model you created to organize the research findings and expands upon it to tell a clear story. By weaving the insights together, you make the research more actionable and not just a series of bulleted facts.

ENGAGES THE READER

Second, a book is nice to look at. It keeps people engaged in the work. How many times have you seen a PowerPoint with bar graphs and started to zone out? A book makes your research dynamic – no more boring presentations.

STANDS OUT

Finally, a book is something unique. It's something you can hold. It's a difference maker. A book is something that can be passed around in a client's office and really stand out. This means that not only will people pay attention to your work, but it will also be a lot easier to socialize the findings in the organization. You can literally get everyone on the same page.

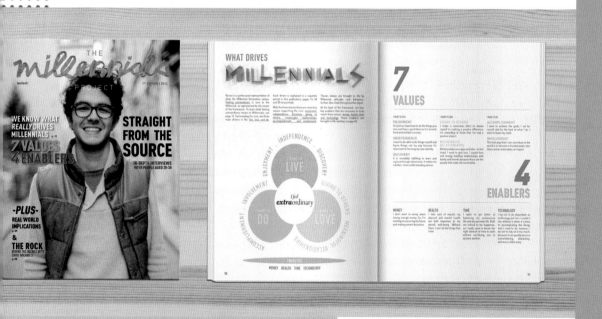

LOOK FOR INSPIRATION

It helps to start by giving yourself some inspiration. Creating a mood board, or a collage of design and aesthetic ideas, can help you transition from a jumble of content to a first draft. You can find the elements to include on your mood board anywhere – but some popular options are Pinterest, Designspiration, and Dribbble. It's important when you gather pieces for the mood board to consider all the elements within your design, so be thinking about colors, typefaces, graphic elements, and photographs – whatever you think is needed to have a clear vision of your project.

MOOD BOARD

We created this mood board to establish the design direction for this book.

THUMBNAIL LAYOUT

Outline your book using thumbnails to plan spreads and layouts.

MAKE AN OUTLINE

After developing your visual direction, it's good to build an outline of your content. This outline usually consists of three basic parts: 1) up-front content, which would be things like your big ideas and research methods; 2) the model content; and 3) any next steps or additional details. Mapping out this content helps you understand the types of pages that will exist within your book. How many spreads do I need to divide up different sections? How many portions of the model are there, and how will I split them up? Creating an outline helps you consider all the possible directions for pacing within your book and determine the best path forward.

CREATE LAYOUTS

Now that you know what you want the book to look like and the order of the content, you can map out how each type of page should be structured. Start by creating various small sketches to immediately determine what ideas will work, and which ones won't. Then bring them into the computer.

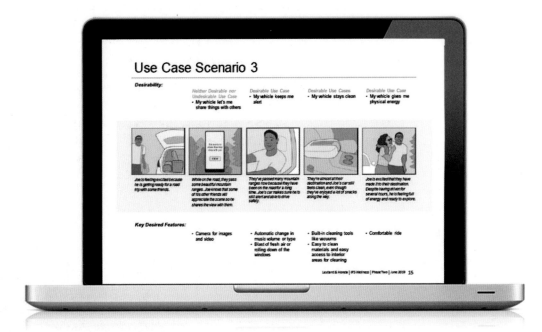

ADOBE INDESIGN

For book layouts, Adobe InDesign really works best. Grab all the content from the longest section and start experimenting with layout. How big should the headers be? How much space should there be between paragraphs? Then, settle it all by creating a grid system, paragraph styles, and appropriate master pages.

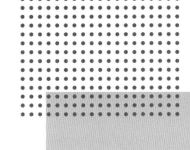

FIND IMAGERY

Your next task is to gather all the elements you need to fill the book. This mostly consists of finding appropriate imagery. Depending on the level of detail in your research, you might be focused on emotional imagery of people or sensory imagery of products and experiences. Either way, finding the right images is key to bringing your research to life. You can get some good ideas on what to include by looking at stimulus words and images participants selected during the study. From there, you'll spend a lot of time scouring the internet to find the visuals you want. As practitioners, we recommend using free resources like Unsplash, Pexels, or Canva photos for emotional imagery and then Pinterest or Dribbble for sensory imagery. Don't be discouraged if this takes a while. The more books you make, the easier it will be to find what you need.

SENSORY IMAGERY

A Pinterest board showing product imagery to describe a Purposeful product.

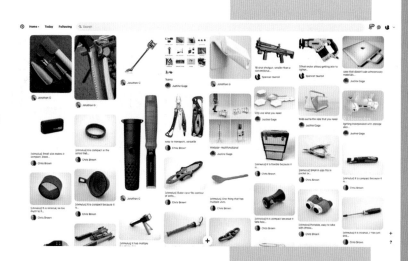

   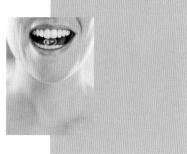

EXPERIENTIAL IMAGERY

Experiential imagery usually has people engaged in the context of an experience. It is intended to evoke ideal emotional states.

HAVE FUN!

Now, pull everything together and play! Once you have all the images you need and your template set up, you can start putting the full book together. Following your template is the best way to start, but remember that design is a fluid process. If something isn't working, change it! If you aren't excited about it, try something different! The ultimate goal is to help readers understand your research and become passionate about it. If your book isn't making that happen, work at it until it does. Be creative. Have fun. Use your good visual design sense to make an impact.

BEAUTIFUL RESEARCH

Pictured above and on the facing page is a book we made to engage the board members of the Ohio Food Bank to understand the perceptions of people on food assistance.

GOALS & OBJECTIVES

TABLE OF CONTENTS

RESEARCH METHOD

WHO WE TALKED TO

BIG IDEAS

USER SEGMENTS & DETAIL

QUALIFYING CRITERIA

PERCEPTIONS

CREATE STORYBOARDS

A storyboard is the visual representation of an experience as an illustrated narrative to frame opportunities, concepts, scenarios, or interactions. There are three reasons to make storyboards:

UNDERSTAND THE CONTEXT OF THE EXPERIENCE

The sequential nature of storyboards allows the design team to see what leads to an event and the impacts afterward. Storyboards can show cause and effect, both in the process as well as the effect on the people emotionally. Storyboards help illustrate natural flow and realistic use cases to ensure that the design team takes all relevant factors into account when they design.

BUILD EMPATHY WITH USERS

Show the personal impact. Make characters' goals and aspirations a part of the story so your audience is aware of their motivations. Illustrate emotional outcomes in addition to issues, limitations, or benefits of solutions. The storyboard should build empathy and clarity about real problems and illustrate the effect on the person, rather than limitations of a product, service, or system. The viewer needs to be engaged in order to relate to the users' point of view and care about what happens to them.

EVALUATE IDEAS

Storyboards are a low-cost way to show consumers a concept that they can react to in order to understand its overall desirability, as well as assess individual features. The level of fidelity will dictate how specific their feedback is. With a low-fidelity storyboard, participants will be able to articulate if an idea is useful or desirable to them. A high-fidelity storyboard will let them respond with a greater level of detail, even uncovering potential usability issues.

1. Looks like Dan Smith is calling... Probably about this rate increase.
Call from Dan Smith

2. Hi Dan. How is your daughter doing?
She's fine. Hey I am calling because my rate went up. Can you tell me why that is?

3. THE AGENT ACCESSES THE CUSTOMER SCREEN
It looks like your Promise discount dropped. I can get that rate for you again if we add your home. Would you like me to do that now?

4. Most of your information is already prefilled. I just have one or two more questions. We can bind now and you can e-sign on your phone.
Great! Let's do it now.

5. Oh no! I put that new payment on the wrong card! I hope it's not too late to change it.

6. Hi Mr. Smith! Is there anything I can do for you? I see your agent just added a policy.
Yes! I need to change the card being billed.

7. No problem. We can make that change now.
GREAT!

8. THE AGENT RECIEVES NOTIFICATION....

HOW TO MAKE A STORYBOARD

1. WRITE A SCRIPT

Below is a script describing a concept for a digital wallet. The story concentrates on the benefits to the user and suggests some key features of the software. It is broken into six discrete sections that can be used to establish the structure of a clear and focused story.

At the mall, our user deliberates on which store she should enter.

- As she nears the entrance, her digital wallet app alerts her that she has a gift card to a store it has detected near her GPS location. Happy she was informed, she chooses to shop at the store she has a gift card for.

- She surveys the store, noting items she is interested in but reminding herself to stick to her budget of $50.

- As she approaches a rack of clothes, her digital wallet app syncs with her GPS location and retrieves a relevant coupon from its database of available offers. She is pleased that her app unexpectedly found the coupon automatically.

- She checks her app and notes that it has taken the budget she set up earlier and added the store gift card and coupon it had pulled up earlier, showing her the total amount she has available to spend. Because of this, she notes that she is able to buy both of the items she is interested in, instead of just one.

- As she checks out, using her app to pay, she observes that the app has presented the gift card and coupon first before using her stored credit card to pay the remainder based on her GPS location. She also notices that although she rarely uses the store credit card, because she has used it at the location over time, the app knows to suggest it first.

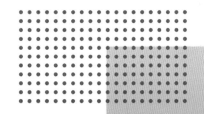

2. PLAN THE ARTWORK

Thumbnail sketches help to plan how the script translates to illustrations of the action.

3. FINALIZE THE STORYBOARD

These frames were created by drawing over digital photos staged by the artist.

CHAPTER 10 REVIEW

MODEL EXPERIENCES

Models tell the desired experience story on a single page.

DESIGN SOURCEBOOKS

Books bring the desired experience story to life in detail.

CREATE STORYBOARDS

Storyboards illustrate what will be produced to deliver the ideal experience.

USING THE PRINCIPLES

RELEVANT

Answers the research questions.

ASPIRATIONAL

Engages the reader/ audience with a story of the desired future.

HOLISTIC

Visualizes the connections between the object of study and the desired outcome of the experience.

RIGOROUS

Represents the patterns in the data.

ACTIONABLE

Describes research findings in a clear and structured way.

VISUAL

Engages the reader with imagery.

WHAT YOU CAN DO NEXT

Explore the relationship between an ideal experience model, a book, and a storyboard. Think about your ideal dining out experience.

- How do you want to feel as a result of your dining out experience (emotions)? What does the restaurant have to do to make you feel this way (benefits)? How do you want those benefits delivered (features)?

- Create a diagram (model) that describes your ideal story.

- Search for images to represent each experiential element.

- Think about a solution that will deliver the ideal experience and create a storyboard that describes it.

APPENDIX

CHAPTER	Relevant	Aspirational	Holistic
1 Making Experiences Actionable		Aspirations, desires, or what people wish for are the high-level outcomes of the Anatomy of an Ideal Experience Framework.	The Anatomy of an Ideal Experience Framework describes complete experiences and connects them to things in the world.
2 Choosing a Research Approach	Research outputs need to connect to the greater goal your design needs to accomplish.		
3 Finding Your Target User	You want to study the people who will actually buy and use what you design.		
4 Having Effective Conversations	The questions you ask must connect to your research objectives. Be intentional with your questions.		
5 Capturing Clear Data			
6 Describing Experiences with Stimuli	What you ask people to make needs to relate to the situation where it will be used.	Ideal Experience collaging is focused on understanding what people wish for. Sensory Cue collaging concentrates on defining the ideal thing.	These tools give you the ability to see the big picture of a current or desired experience and the details of the thing you are designing.
7 Understanding the Situations of Use	Describes the situation of use.	Try to understand what people want to happen along with what is happening today.	
8 Conducting Research	Pilot testing ensures the research objectives will be addressed.		
9 Finding the Big Ideas			Coding groups data into emotions, benefits, features, and sensory cues.
10 Telling the Story of the Future	Answers the research questions.	Engaging story of the desired future.	Visualizes the connections between the thing and the desired outcome of the experience.

Rigorous	Actionable	Visual
	Sensory cues are concrete.	Different types of imagery can be used to describe each of the four components of the Anatomy of an Ideal Experience Framework.
		You want to plan for deliverables that people want to pick up and read.
If you study the wrong people you will design the wrong thing. The people you study are the foundation of your research.		
It's easy to lead the witness. Don't conduct interviews in a way that creates bias. You want to get to the truth.		
This is a data-driven process. You don't want to ground your design in inaccurate data. Notes must accurately reflect what occurred in your research.		
	Sensory cues are concrete.	Images are used to describe experiences and things.
Capturing data in context requires planning.	Identifies situations and outcomes	Telling a story about context requires pictures and video. Observation is a visual act.
Refining your plan before you collect data allows you to have a repeatable process and identify patterns.		
Identifying patterns in your data that occur across multiple participants ensures your findings are representative of the real world.		When analyzing data from projective techniques, you are identifying what the stimuli mean. Putting stimulus data on theme sheets helps organize the story based upon a common visual.
Represents the patterns in the data.	Describes research findings in a clear and structured way.	Engages the reader with imagery.

CHAPTER/SECTION	INTRODUCTION	SUMMARY
1 A User-Driven Perspective on Design Thinking	There are many points of view on the design thinking process. You will learn how we think about it.	Focus on defining value, aligning teams on what people want, directing creativity toward solving problems grounded in desired experiences, prototyping in a way that communicates experientially, and measuring ideas based upon what people find valuable.
Defining Value: What People Really Want	You will learn to do research that helps you generate ideas. For your ideas to be successful other people need to find them valuable. Just as there are steps in the design thinking process, there are structured steps in the first stage of that process. This is our process. This book will teach you those steps.	Utilize a structured process to defining value. The rest of the book explains how to master this process.
Ideal Experience Research	You need to understand what people value in a way that informs your designs. We utilize a structured framework to help you think about and describe experiences in an actionable way. It's patented.	Think experientially. Connect the dots between what you make and how it makes people feel.
2 Define Your Research Objectives	As we mentioned in the introduction, your design needs to accomplish a greater goal. Typically this is a business result. In order to design something that delivers a meaningful experience, you need to understand many things. This will inevitably lead to questions you need answers to. These questions are the goals for your research.	It's important to think about the kind of information you will need to answer your research questions. Research can generate many different types of information and insight.
Select a Research Approach	There are many ways to get information from people.	Each research approach generates specific types of information. Your research methodology choices need to generate answers to your research questions.
Consider the End Deliverable	You need to think about the type of story you want to tell at the end of your research.	The methodology choices you make impact the types of deliverables you can create. Once your research is over, you are stuck with the information you generated. Make sure you have the information you need for the type of deliverable you plan to create.

CHAPTER/SECTION	INTRODUCTION	SUMMARY
3 Identify Participation Criteria	You need to make sure that you study the kind of people who will actually use what you design, aka your target audience. Your research needs to be credible in order for other people to believe your conclusions. If you study the right people, it will ultimately help you justify your design decisions.	You never want to design anything without a target audience in mind. The key factors to consider when describing your target participants are demographics, category engagement, attitude or mindset, and articulation.
Create a Screener	You want to make a tool that helps you determine if someone is part of your target audience and a good research participant. If a person is familiar with what you are designing, they will be able to share their past experiences and aspirations. This will ensure you get useful information.	This is a commonly used tool. Designing a good screener helps establish your credibility with other research disciplines such as market research or consumer insights.
Find Your Participants	You need to come up with a plan to discover the people who are right for your study.	Your research is only as good as the people you study. These people will serve as the foundation for your design decisions. Make sure you have a solid plan for locating them.
4 Formulate Your Questions	The questions you ask a research participant should be directly related to your research objectives. You are going from a few big objectives to a detailed set of questions.	Make sure that your questions align with your research objectives. Be intentional with your questions. Know where you want to go and have a plan. Stick with open-ended questions. Don't bias people by putting the answer to the question in your question.
Create a Discussion Guide	You want to have a structured plan for how you do your interviews. This guide puts all of your interview questions in a sequence that flows.	Use this tool to structure your interview. Make sure your questions have a logical flow that is easy for your participants to follow. Timing is critical, so make sure you address it in your guide. This guide enables you to have a repeatable process so that you can find patterns in your data.
Conduct Interviews	Moderation, or guiding a discussion, is a skill that you develop over the course of many conversations. Everyone has their own unique approach, but it takes a lot of practice to discover your own approach that is not only effective at getting the data you need but also authentic to who you are.	Make people comfortable. A discussion guide is a plan, not a script, so keep your research objectives in mind as you conduct interviews. Be flexible but consistent in your discussions. Don't bias people. Bring a clock so you can stay on time. Be yourself.

CHAPTER/SECTION		INTRODUCTION	SUMMARY
5	Structure Your Data	When you execute your research approach, you will generate data. It's important to have a plan for how you will capture and organize it.	Have a plan for how you will capture and organize your data.
	Use a Spreadsheet Tool	Spreadsheet software such as Microsoft Excel or Google Sheets is a critical tool for design research.	Don't wait to do this. Chapter 9 depends on it.
	Take Good Notes	Once your research fielding is complete, this is what you will be using to tell your story.	A good note is complete, discrete, relevant, non-judgmental, and unbiased.
6	Understand the Applications of Collaging	This tool can capture many different types of information.	Choose a collaging approach that aligns with your research objectives.
	Prepare Collage Exercises	A collage activity is comprised of a canvas and stimuli.	Each type of exercise requires a different canvas and stimulus customized to your research effort.
	Conduct Collage Exercises	You need to know how to present these activities to people and how to moderate the explanation of what is made.	The moderation questions have a different focus for each approach, but they can use a similar note template.
7	Approaches to Contextual Inquiry	There are many ways to understand where your design will live and what will happen around it. These are a few methods we use most often.	Determine if it makes more sense to capture moments or processes. Decide what is the best way to get that information: do it yourself or have your participants do it for you.
	Know Your Documentation Options	Plan on telling your story in your deliverable.	Video and photography are important tools for capturing context. Self-documentation tools allow you to get this information without being there.
	Conduct an Efficient & Effective Inquiry	Observations are an important source of data. Capturing data in context requires planning.	Develop an observation guide. Be thoughtful about the imagery you capture. Think about how you will take notes in context.

CHAPTER/SECTION		INTRODUCTION	SUMMARY
8	Prepare for the Study	Never underestimate how important it is to be ready when you show up in someone else's world.	Eliminate the distractions you can control.
	Finalize Your Setup	Make a list of everything you need to have ready and packed before you go. Be professional.	There are many things to think about in an interview, including consent, technology, data capture, and materials. Moderation is your key focus at this time.
	Solidify the Approach	Test your research methodology to make sure it works.	Every research methodology needs to be refined before data is collected. In order to have a repeatable process, you can't modify your approach as you go.
9	Code the Data	Group similar ideas from different participants together.	Codes describe the various stories that live in the data. Creating and using codes enables you to group similar ideas together.
	Identify Themes	Summarize similar ideas from different participants.	Themes are singular insights formed from 25% or more of your participants. These are the building blocks of your story.
	Synthesize Themes	Group summarized ideas into buckets.	Bucketing organizes your themes into chapters. Reducing the components in your story enables you to build a one-page framework.
10	Model Experiences	Organize insights into a one-page framework.	Models tell the desired experience story on a single page.
	Design Sourcebooks	Structure a deliverable that explains what you have learned in your research.	Books bring the desired experience story to life in detail.
	Create Storyboards	Tell the story of the future.	Storyboards illustrate what will be produced to deliver the ideal experience.

INDEX

comfort of, 85
consent forms for, 186
identification system for, 185
participant ID numbers, 100, 198, 199
participation criteria for, 62–63
recruiting, 68
respect for, 85, 90
screeners for, 64
Research study(-ies), 21, 180–193
finalizing set-up for, 184–187
flexibility and understanding of, 86
participation criteria for, 62–63
pilot testing for, 188–189
preparing for, 182, 193
user research principles, 180, 190
Respect, for research participants, 85, 90
Rigorous research, 13

Scents, 127, 136–137
Scope of project, 87, 107
Screeners, 64–68
Screening questions, 66–67
Scripts, 80, 83, 246
Segments, customer, 63
Self-documentation, 47
apps and tools for, 169
in contextual inquiries, 162
information captured by, 45, 51
questions for, 175
Self-expression, 45
Self-representation, 85
Sensory cues:
defined, 42, 50
deliverables on, 54–55
design application of, 24–25, 42, 50

examples, 32–33
in ideal experiences, 23, 230–231
methods of examining, 51
multisensory stimuli for, 130–135
thinking about, 32–33
Sensory cue collaging:
applications of, 116–117
build in, 144–145
canvases for, 119–121, 125
choosing features for, 122–123
"Ideal Me" activity for, 143–144
moderation of, 148–150
multisensory stimuli kits for, 130–140
note-taking in, 151
virtual, 140
Sensory cue frameworks, 55
Sensory cue words, 130–131, 145
Sensory images, 241
Sequencing, of questions, 81–83
Services:
formulating questions about, 77
research approaches examining, 45
Signals, stimulus kits for, 136–137
Situational outcomes, collaging to understand, 115
Situations of use, understanding, 115. See also Contextual inquiry
Sketches, model, 232
Solutions, 171, 212, 219
Sorting data:
for coding, 199
for theming, 197, 204–205
Sounds, 127, 136–137
Spreadsheets, 104, 199, 205, 207, 208

Stimuli, 126–140
editing groups of, 139
for emotions, 128–129
for experience collaging, 129
for features and sensory cues, 130–135
grouping, 139
in multisensory stimulus kits, 138–140
numbering, 140
presenting, to participants, 145
survey outputs as, 169
Stimulus kits for collaging. See also Multisensory stimulus kits
building, 126–127
finalizing set-up with, 187
information elicited by, 51
Stimulus numbers, on theme sheet, 210
Storyboards, 244–247
Storytelling, 225–251
with design sourcebooks, 236–243
with models, 228–235
preparing for, 251
relationships between methods of, 251
with storyboards, 244–247
user research principles, 225, 248–249
Supplies, finalizing, 185
Surveys, 123, 169
Synthesizing themes, 197, 216–220

Tags, data, 101, 199
Target user, 60–73
creating screeners, 64–67
finding research participants, 68
identifying participation criteria, 62–63